THE SPIRITUAL JOURNEY

Towards an Indian Christian Spirituality

THE SPIRITUAL JOURNEY
Towards an Indian Christian Spirituality

S. Painadath SJ

ISPCK
2007

The Spiritual Journey : Towards an Indian Christian Spirituality—
Published by the Rev. Dr. Ashish Amos of the Indian Society for
Promoting Christian Knowledge (ISPCK), Post Box 1585,
Kashmere Gate, Delhi-110006.

© Author, 2006

Revised edition, 2007

Cover design : NAVEEN

ISBN: 81-7214-898-4

Laser typeset at
ISPCK, Post Box 1585, 1654 Madarsa Road, Kashmere Gate,
Delhi-110006 • *Tel:* 23866323
e-mail: ashish@ispck.org.in • mail@ispck.org.in
website: www.ispck.org.in
Printed at Cambridge Press, Kashmere Gate, Delhi-110006.

CONTENTS

CONTENTS

PREFACE

We live in a new epoch of the spiritual evolution of humanity. One of the features that characterises this newness is the global quest for authentic spiritual experiences. A mystical wind blows over the world today crossing all boundaries of religions and cultures. Sensitivity to the ultimate mystery is awakened in scientists and artists; a sense of eco-harmony is alerted in those engaged in social service and political commitment. Through and beyond, and even independent of, the traditional forms of religiosity evolves an ardent quest for a mystical experience of the Divine. How could Christian faith, with a deep insertion to India's spiritual heritage, respond to this quest? – this is the question that we take up for theological reflection in this book.

After locating certain characteristics of the Asian spiritual heritage, the basic structure of mystical introspection is described. With this we make an attempt to explore the deeper dimensions of the inner journey of Jesus. Then we look into the divinisation process that takes place deep within us in consequence of the salvific experience of Jesus. Further we reflect on how the inner contemplative experience motivates commitment to liberative action. In these five chapters on mystical experience the main insight is this: God-in-Christ is the true *subject* of our life. The Gospel according to John together with some Upanishads accompany us on this inner spiritual journey. An encounter between Christian faith and Upanishadic Vedanta is the inner dynamism of this spiritual pursuit.

In the subsequent three chapters the effects of the mystical perspective on the Christian understanding of the mystery of the Divine as well the social and ecological consequences in spiritual life are taken up for reflection. A specific aspect of the Christian mystical experience is that the God-with-us in Christ is the God who suffers with us and transforms everything to a new creation. This perspective raises a radical social demand, which is illustrated with the meal-fellowship of Jesus. The other is the ecological consequence which is clarified in relation to the mystery of the Eucharist, the sacrament of the mother earth.

India's spiritual heritage is endowed with deep mystical experiences. Below the surface of religious rituals and social customs there are the deep undercurrents of mystical experience in the Indian heritage. These are articulated in the Upanishads of the sages and in the devotional hymns of the bhakti saints. The revelation of the divine Word and the grace of the divine Spirit have to be discerned in them. Any authentic Christian spirituality in this country has to be nourished by these mystical well-springs. Such an integration would be in line with the creative process that the Church Fathers of the 2nd and 3rd centuries initiated in the Greco-Roman world. In spiritual encounter with the mystical experiences and religious symbols of the milieu they developed Christian theology and spirituality. This process has to continue with responsible freedom and creativity in the local Churches all over the world, definitely in India, the womb of great World Religions.

My basic concern in sharing these reflections is to awaken the *mystic* and alert the *prophet* in the Church in dialogue with the Scriptural sources of Christian faith and Indian spirituality. My perspectives specifically on inter-religious dialogue are offered in the companion volume: *We are Co-pilgrims, Towards a Culture of Inter-religious Harmony*, ISPCK, Delhi 2006.

I am grateful to ISPCK for publishing the book.

Sebastian Painadath SJ
Sameeksha,
Centre for Indian Spirituality,
Kalady 683574,India
spainadath@gmail.com

1

THE ASIAN HERITAGE

Asia is a great womb of the world's spiritual heritage. Tribals and nomads have been the primal bearers of Asian spiritual consciousness. Gradually, scriptures evolved articulating the spiritual pilgrimage of humanity. The various stages of this evolution are still vibrantly present in the religions and cultures of Asia. The rich diversity of religious life is a fascinating reality on this vast continent. We Asians, by nature, resonate with diversity and hence we resist religious absolutism and cultural uniformism. Diversity is beauty, not only in nature but also in culture. Diversity of cultures shows quality of life; plurality of religions means richness of divine grace. "Diversity is not something to be regretted and abolished, but to be rejoiced over and promoted, since it represents richness and strength. The test of true harmony is the acceptance of diversity as richness."[1] Respect for the otherness of the other is the matrix of the Asian religious psyche. The spiritual source of this respect is a contemplative perception of reality; the expression of it is the all-embracing compassionate attitude to living beings. Pope Paul VI perceived this: Asia is a continent, the past history of whose people manifests "the sense of spiritual values dominating the thoughts of their sages and the lives of their vast multitudes."[2]

Aspects of Asian Spirituality

The Asian spiritual sensitivity has the following characteristics:

---

[1] FABC-BIRA. IV/11,1988, No.15.
[2] FABC-Plenary Assembly II, 1978, Final Statement, Nos. 7,30.

1. A sense of **mystery** permeates all attitudes to life and reality in Asia. Deep within the consciousness one is gripped by the unfathomable mystery that vibrates in the entire cosmos. With this sense of mystery one speaks of reality as void (*sunya*), which actually means flux (*svi* = expand), or as the fullness (*poorna*), that permeates everything. This gives rise to the mystical perception of the immanent power of harmony in the universe. "There is an ineffable universal rhythm that unifies everything into an organic whole which binds together pluralistic reality. The Asian sages perceived this unifying principle of harmony as Tao, Rta, and Dharma."[3] The primary awareness of the Divine in the life of an Asian, is that of the abysmal mystery. "A contemplative awakening to the all-pervading and all-transcending mystery of the Divine is a hallmark of Asian spirituality."[4] Hence an Asian seeker is reluctant to name the Divine; if named at all, that name will be withdrawn in the next breath, and it will be said: I do not how to speak about it![5] No categorical name-and-form of the Divine can exhaustively and definitely express the absolutely transcendent mystery of the Divine. Hence 'no particular religion can raise the claim of being the norm for all others'.[6] Only in terms of the sensitivity to this mystery dimension can one understand the manifold expressions of Asian religiosity.

2. The contemplative perception of reality gives rise to a **holistic understanding** of humanity and cosmos. The entire universe is seen as one well-knit organism. The divine power permeates all realities and binds them together in the one process of life. All things are evolving together like branches of a tree, like members of one body, like movements of dancing. Reality is in a constant flux, like the flow of a river in which millions of drops dance in compenetration. There is nothing ultimately static in this universe: reality is vibration. There is nothing isolated in this world: reality is relational. Everything is bound with everything else on a universal

---

[3] FABC-BIRA. V,1995, No.1
[4] FABC-FEISA. I, 1994, Nos 7.2.3.
[5] Kena Upanishad,1,3.
[6] FABC-FEISA. V,1995, No.6.

web. These are the mystical insights of the great seers (*rishis*) of Asia. "Asian religions always perceived in cosmos and history a process towards greater integration."[7]

3. Not only the perception of reality but its expression too is holistic in Asia. Hence **myths** play a decisive role in shaping the religious psyche of Asians. Myths are the symbolic articulations of the deepest movements of the psyche, personal as well as cultural.[8] A contemplative awakening to reality sets in motion certain stirrings deep within the person or community. These are articulated through myths, which unfold through sagas and stories, dance and music, sculptures and architecture, festivals and ecstatic movements. The Asian psyche does not resonate with a dominantly conceptual process of the analytical mind and hence it resists dogmatic formulations and normative regulations of any religious authority. We Asians like to dance out our religious experience in harmony with the entire cosmos and in tune with the Divine. The whole universe is a dance, ultimately the dance of the Divine; this is the meaning of the symbol of the dancing Siva (*Nataraja*).

4. Personal **spiritual experience** (*anubhava*) is normative (*pramana*) in the growth of an individual and in the evolution of a community. Since reality is a mystery, access to it has to be a matter of personal search. Asians are basically seekers: spiritual pilgrims in a relentless quest for Truth. "Life is perceived in Asia as an ongoing journey. What gives ultimate meaning to life is the spiritual pilgrimage in pursuit of Truth, Harmony, the Divine.[9] In this pilgrimage each one shares one's experience with others. "We join other believers on the pilgrimage beyond, celebrating our interdependence and our oneness before the ever-greater Mystery."[10] It is this contemplative attitude that makes Asians tolerant towards the diversity of Truth-perceptions in religions. A

---

[7] FABC-FEISA. I, 1994, Nos.7.2.4

[8] Panikkar, Raimundo, Myth Faith and Hermeneutics, Asian Trading Corporation, Bangalore, 1983, 40-64.

[9] FABC-FEISA. I, 1994, Nos. 7.1.1.

[10] FABC-BIRA. IV/12, 1991, No.40.

person in his/her search can be a genuine seeker only in an atmosphere of being respected, not dominated, of being accepted, not suppressed. *Ekam sat vipra bahudha vadanti*: Truth is one, those who perceive it speak of it in diverse ways - this Vedic axiom expresses the basic attitude of Asian seekers.[11]

5. Intense **spiritual discipline** is a prerequisite in spirituality. Asian traditions unfold the need of ascetical practices and contemplative silence in pursuit of Truth. The seeker (*sadhaka*) experiences his / her body as the temple of God, and hence discipline of the body, dietary regulations and meditative postures are inevitable elements of spiritual life. A certain simplicity of life style and a genuine closeness to nature characterize authentic spiritual seekers in Asia. "We must safeguard the wealth of contemplation and interiority that has been ours so as to be able to offer these values as precious gifts to the Church, for without contemplation and prayer human society loses its way; and without contact with the living God, it is not even possible to safeguard humanity."[12] A life that evolves out of contemplative pursuits is a life of openness to Truth and respect for the diversity of Truth-perceptions, a life of compassion towards all beings and commitment to integral harmony. However the spiritual masters of Asia emphasize that ultimately this contemplative introspection is a gift from the divine centre of being. The Divine can be intuited only in the divine light, which is a gift of grace.[13] All spiritual pursuits are a process of opening our self to the divine Self, surrendering our soul to the Holy Spirit, tuning the *atma* with the *Atma*.

6. In this inner contemplative process one becomes aware of the Divine as the **ultimate subject** of life process. In the mystical consciousness one wakes to the realization that God is the true subject of our being. The entire reality is in fact an outpouring of the divine energy, articulation of the divine vibration in the cosmos, manifestation of the divine love in the world, unfolding of the divine

---

[11] Rig Veda, 1.164.46.
[12] FABC-Plenary Assembly II, 1978, Final Statement, Nos. 9, 13.
[13] Bhagavad Gita,11:8.

root through the cosmic tree. Such mystical symbols cannot just be interpreted through the analytical framework of the reasoning mind; they rather point to a deeper level of consciousness in which one experiences a mystical oneness with the Divine and with all beings in the Divine. It is a foretaste of the eschatological reality of 'God being all in all'. Asian sages have an insight into this universal *theophany*, and hence they describe creation and history in terms of a progressive unfolding of the divine Spirit in the universe.[14] Contemplation is 'openness to the mystery of God's saving action in history'.[15]

7. The sense of the Divine as incomprehensible mystery and all-pervading presence gives rise to a sensitivity to **harmony**. Cultures are recognised in their specific creativity and religions are respected in their particular perception of the Absolute. All religions are seen as ways to the liberating experience of the Divine. Tolerance towards religions is a hallmark of the Asian religious culture. Followers of different religions live in harmony in good neighbourly relationship (except in places where politics or religious fundamentalism poison the minds). Harmony does not mean ignoring the differences. On the contrary, differences are being respected while the deeper unity is perceived. Respect the otherness of the other and recognise what unifies all – this is the principle of harmony in Asia. Consequently religions from the primal forms to the highest mystical pursuits flourish side by side in Asian countries.

8. This holistic vision of reality gives rise to a **compassionate attitude** to all beings. As one experiences oneself in harmony with the entire cosmic reality in the divine process, one's heart is filled with a loving concern for the integral welfare of all beings. No one can be considered a stranger to oneself, and the suffering of the other becomes one's own suffering. All Asian religions uphold compassion (*karuna, daya, rachem*) as the hallmark of a truly

---

[14] Aurobindo, Man and the Evolution, in: The Life Divine, Pondicherry, 1977, 824-847

[15] FABC-BIRA. III, 1982, No. 6,

spiritual person. Genuine compassion consists in suffering with the other and participating in the struggles of the other for overcoming the suffering. Compassion is a transformative attitude to life. The Asian sense of compassion embraces not only human world but also the animal world as well as the wide range of the wounded earth. Hence ecological concerns are integral elements of spirituality in Asia.

Since this contemplative - introspective and holistic - grasp of reality expressed in a compassionate attitude to life is characteristic of the Asian psyche, Christian communities have to revitalize the contemplative dimension of faith experience in dialogue with believers of other religions if they have to bear credible witness to Christ on this continent. Life in the Spirit is an inner pilgrimage: unto an inner realisation of the transforming presence of the divine Spirit and creative collaboration with the Spirit in the world. Mystical introspection enlightens prophetic commitment; and commitment in turn deepens introspection. This dialectics is at the core of spirituality as well as of theology in Asia. Any authentic reflection on faith experience presupposes a genuine experience of the Divine in the human. "In the midst of the peoples of Asia, whose cultures hold contemplative dimension in the highest regard..., we would have a message for Asia only when our Asian sisters and brothers see in us the marks of God-realized persons. Credibility is the fruit of authenticity."[16]

(The FABC Documents have been complied in the following volumes: Vol. I G.B. Rosales and C.G. Arevalo SJ (ed), For all the Peoples of Asia, Vols II-III. Franz-Josef Eilers SVD, (ed), For all the Peoples of Asia, Claretian Publ. Quezon, Philippines/ Bangalore, India 1987 / 1997).

---

[16] FABC. Plenary Assembly V, 1994, Final Statement, Nos. 9.2.

2

THE INWARD JOURNEY

On the inward spiritual journey Asian sages as well as Christian mystics describe various levels of consciousness. One starts with the upper level of consciousness and slowly moves to the deeper spheres. It is like getting down into a well or diving into the depths of the sea, like peeling an onion or like moving from the periphery of the circle to its centre, from the rim of a wheel to its hub. This is a centripetal movement that cuts through various concentric circles. The English word meditation comes from the Latin verb *meditari*, which means to go to the centre. The Sanskrit word for meditation is *dhyana*, which literally means journey (*yana*) to the intuitive perception (*dhi, buddhi*). The inward journey is a spiritual pilgrimage to the divine centre of one's being.

The Upanishadic masters (800–300 BC) speak of three levels of consciousness: the wakeful level (*jagrit*) controlled by the mind (*manah*), the dream state (*swapna*) present in the psyche (*chittah*) and the mystical realm (*sushupti*) awakened in the intuitive faculty (*buddhi*)

Beyond the senses there is the mind (*manah*)
Beyond the mind there is the intuitive organ (*buddhi*)
Beyond the *buddhi* is the inner self (*atman*)

(Katha Up 3,10)

The Mental Sphere (*manah*)

This is the surface level of awareness; from morning till night one is at this level. *I* am constantly encountering a *thou* or an *it*, persons or things. What steers this extrovert movement is the mind (*manah*). Within the mind there is a twofold activity: to know and to will.

Hence the mind is full of thoughts and feelings. Mind can understand something only in as much as the latter is objectified. Mind operates in a subject-object structure. Even if *I* am trying to understand myself, I have to objectify myself: I have to take myself in the hand. Mind objectifies everything including God. In this extrovert process of the mind a sense of I-and-mine feeling (*ahamkara*) evolves. This sense of the ego (*aham*) is something constitutive of the human mind. Everyone needs a healthy sense of ego to accept oneself and to affirm oneself in relation to persons and things. It is through ego that one realises one's subjectivity. *I* encounter the *thou* and return to myself enriched by the *thou*. Through the *thou*, *I* become truly *I*. All socio-cultural-religious activities take place at this upper level of awareness.

The Psychic State (*chittah*)

The actions and reactions at the mental level are controlled by inner-psychic factors. These evolve out of the hidden realms of the sub-conscious. This inner *womb* of the psyche is shaped by one's own biography and also through the evolutionary process of humanity. Several unexpressed emotions and unarticulated thoughts are preserved within this inner recess. Memories of the past – personal as well as collective – are stored in this inner warehouse. Some of these elements surface in dreams. Several factors of the collective unconscious find expression in myths and legends. In them we recognise the collective archetypes emerging from the deeper realms of our psyche. Hence acquaintance with the symbols and stories of myths can be a great help for psychic integration. Modern psychology tries to unearth and interpret some of the hidden processes in the psyche. However we will never succeed understanding ourselves fully. We are a mystery to ourselves. An introspection into the psyche will make us realise that we are not just isolated individuals, but deeply related to one another: we are parts of an evolving totality. This is the basic insight contained in the idea of rebirth, prevalent in the tribal and Indic religions.

The Intuitive Consciousness (*buddhi*)

When one dives into the levels below the psyche one is brought to a deeper level of consciousness, which may be called transcendental perception or mystical consciousness. Some like to call it meta-consciousness or super-consciousness. It is at this level that one experiences one's true self in union with the absolute Self. Here one realises one's true identity in harmony with the totality of reality. Here one is brought to the boundary of individual consciousness and experiences the infinite horizons unto which one is existentially open. This is entry to the inner cave of the heart. That by which this introspection takes place is called *buddhi*, the intuitive faculty of perception. Mystics and sages of all times and religions speak of this inner spiritual organ. Buddhi is the door to mystical consciousness. Christian mystics describe it as *sensus mysticus, scintilla animae, apex mentis, the inner eye* (Augustine) , *the third eye* (Richard von St. Victor) or *Seelenfünklein* (Meister Eckhart). Jesus spoke of it as the inner *eye*, the *light within.*(Lk. 11: 34-36). In Indic traditions the symbols for buddhi are *inner eye* (Bhag. Gita), *inner light* (Upanishads) and *lotus of the heart* (Vedas).[1]

Mind and Buddhi

There is therefore a definite distinction between the two types of perception, that of the mind at the upper level of understanding and that of the buddhi at the deeper level of intuition:

- Mind (*mens*) operates within the subject-object polarity: I encounter the thou / it. Buddhi (*intellectus*) transcends this polarity : I and thou / it merge into a unity of transcendental consciousness.

---

[1] "Buddhi as the highest evolute of nature and therefore the nearest to the immortal self is single, simple, one, because its true function is contemplation of the Eternal. As man's highest faculty is directed towards God." Zaehner, Bhagavad Gita, Oxford,1969, 142-3
"The inner light of the buddhi unifies perception." Sankara, Gitabhashya, 4.3.7.

- Mind looks at the structures and qualities of the world, while buddhi contemplates the axis of the world.

- Mind objectifies everything and analyses reality in its individuality and diversity. Buddhi enters into the depth of reality (*intus ire*, intuition) by uniting it with the perceiving subject.

- Through the mind one is driven to the fascinating diversity of things while buddhi delves into the mystery of the unity of reality.

- Mind pursues the logic of reality; buddhi explores the mystique of reality. "How can *He* be known, by whom all this is made known?" – this is the constant search of the buddhi (Brih. Up, 4.5.15).

- Mind speculates on the horizontal level and acquires a conceptual knowledge (*vijnana*) of persons and things, while buddhi contemplates reality in its abysmal depth dimension and attains the intuitive wisdom (*jnana*).

- Through the mind (*ratio*) one reaches objective understanding and communicates it by way of information; in buddhi (*intuitio*) however one is graced with intuitive perception that leads to transformation.

- Mind operates on the principle of duality and classifies everything according to structures and qualities; buddhi unfolds on the principle of unity and contemplates everything in terms of universal inter-relatedness (*dharma/ plan of God*).

- Mental understanding is conditioned by one's standpoint and hence it is always fragmentary; through the intuitive entry into the depth of reality however a new consciousness arises in which one perceives reality holistically.

- Mind deals with the objects conveyed through the exterior or interior senses. Buddhi takes one's consciousness to the *sacred space* within.

- Mind is an evolute of nature (prakriti); buddhi is related to the spirit (purusha).

Revealed and yet dwelling hidden in the cave,
is that which is called the great Atman.
Whatever moves and breathes and blinks
is fixed therein. Know this as being
and also non-being, the passion of all hearts,
transcending all knowledge.
Yet that is to be known – know that

(Mundaka Upanishad 2.2.1)

When the inner light shines forth in the buddhi one looks into the inner recess of reality.[2] What does one see there? Nothing (*sunya*)! Yet this is fullness (*poorna*). This is an ineffable experience. This is entry into the sacred space within. Mystics and sages of different religions struggle to describe this space by using diverse symbols: *cave of the heart* (Mund. Up. 2.2.1), *space of the heart* (Brih. Up. 4.4.22) *city of the Divine* (Chand. Up. 8.1.1) *inner garden* of the soul (Sufis), *interior castle* (Theresa of Avila), *inner space of the spirit* (Meister Eckhart). Jesus spoke of it as the *inner room* in which one truly experiences the Father: "When you pray, go into your inner room (*tamieion*), shut yourself in and pray to your Father who is in the secret place" (Mt. 6,6). When he taught his disciples to invoke God as *Our Father in the heavens*, (*en tois ouranois*) did he not mean the infinite divine space within?

The experience that one makes in this inner space is ineffable. This cannot be fully grasped by the mind nor can it be totally expressed at the level of the language. Mystics of all spiritual traditions basically point to three dimensions of the experience of the relationship between the human self (and the cosmos) and the divine Self: (a) the human is different from the Divine, (*dwaita/ creatureliness*), (b) the human is a particle of the Divine (*visishtadwaita/participation*), and (c) the human is ultimately one

---

[2] "Buddhi is the point at which the human mind is open to the divine light. It is also the point of unification of the personality. It is at this point that we become fully human. If buddhi turns towards the light, it is illumined by the divine light and transmits the light to the manah and the senses. But if buddhi is turned away from the light then the mind is darkened and the personality is divided." Bede Griffiths, Marriage of East and West, Collins, London, 1982, 71..

with the Divine (*adwaita/ mystical union*). Basically one should be open to all these three aspects of experience, for one cannot pre-programme how the Divine directly deals with the human.

An integrated spiritual process demands both an inter-personal encounter with the divine Lord at the mind level and a transpersonal experience of the divine Spirit in buddhi realm. Out of the inter-personal encounter evolves the response of devotional self-surrender (*bhakti*) and out of the experience of oneness comes gnostic contemplation (*jnana*). Out of an integration of both one gets engaged in 'works for the welfare of the world' (*karma*). The basic dynamics of a liberative spirituality is described in the Christian axiom, *be a contemplative in action*, (Ignatius of Loyola) and in the Indian aphorism, *being united with the Divine, get involved in your works*. (Bh. Gita, 2:48).

Who am I?

Who am I? - This is the basic question that resounds throughout the inner spiritual journey. Seekers and sages of all religions constantly ask themselves this question. In fact every religion evolves out of the answer, however fragmentary, which this question finds. Every human person has a particular understanding of himself/herself. This is very much related to the mental perception of oneself. One discovers one's social identity in relation to family and profession, religion and culture, language and nation. But one knows well that these factors do not really define one's genuine spiritual identity; the real root of our being lies elsewhere. One can never fully grasp it. Hence the relentless quest : Where do I come from ? Where are my roots? Who am I? (*ko-aham*)

With this existential question the inner journey takes the seeker to the deeper levels of consciousness. One moves from the mental sphere through the psychic realm into the intuitive awareness of reality. At the mental level (*manah*) one discovers one's identity in exclusion of everything else: I am what I am, because I am not you. Once the consciousness sinks to the intuitive level (*buddhi*) one experiences one's identity in harmony with everything else: I am what I am, because I am one with you. Mind objectifies everything, but buddhi transcends the subject-object polarity.[3]

When the question, *who am I,* is put only at the mind level, the answer surfaces within the conditioning factors of subject-object polarity. But when this question is contemplated at the buddhi level, the answer flashes in from the Ground of being. Sages and seers, mystics and prophets of all religious cultures did have a deeper perception of the real human identity. If we make a meditative reading of their descriptions, we find converging lines in their inner spiritual pursuits as well as a certain coherence in the insights they received though their symbols and concepts vary. The one Light, that enlightens all, shines forth through the buddhi in all human seekers. Hence in spite of the divergence in language and symbols there is an immanent unity of experience in all the seers. Ultimately this means: we have a divine origin, a divine rootedness; we are *divine*!

Know who you are

The Upanishadic sages of India constantly asked the question, who am I? (*ko-aham*, Ait.Up.1.3.11). They were in a relentless search for 'knowing the Knower of all'. (Brih.Up. 4.5.15). They were not content with encountering God at the mental level as thou (*tvam*), but they sought the experience of the Divine as the true Self (*Atman*), as the deepest subject (*kartha*), as the inner mover (*antaryamin*); within this mystical experience they explored their true identity (Brih.Up.1.4.7; 3.7.3). Hence the sage says: "That which is not thought by the mind, that by which the mind thinks, that verily is Brahman, and not what people here adore" (Kena Up.1.6). In this meditative journey into the ultimate depth of reality they realised their true identity in oneness with the ultimate Self: I am Atman; I am Brahman (Brih. Up.4.4.12;3.5.1;1.4.10; Mahanar.Up.158). They felt their body translucent for the divine Light (Tait.Up.1.4.1),

---

[3] "The so called contradictions are such only at the mental level, but are in reality complementary aspects of the Overmind (intuition: truth is hidden beyond words and concepts." (Jules Monchanin, The Christian Approach to Hinduism, in Indian Missiological Bulletin, June 1952.)

their consciousness transparent to the divine Ground (Tait.Up.1.10.1).

Christian mystics too went on an inner journey to discover the deeper self-identity. They experienced the God revealed in Christ as the Spirit within. "The Spirit of Christ, abiding in our heart, makes our spirit realise that we are sons/daughters of God, heirs of God, coheirs of Christ" (Rom. 8:14-17). They experienced the true identity of their self in relation to the Divine. In deep mystical consciousness God is not just a *thou* before us but the Self, the Spirit, within us. This deep oneness is described by Jesus with the image: I am the vine-stock, you are the branches (Jn.15:5). Between the vine-stock and the branches there is a deep oneness; ultimately there is no difference between the stem and the branches. Paul experienced the depth of this consciousness and cried out : "I live, not I, Christ lives in me" (Gal. 2:20). He experienced Christ as the true Self of his self. The Spirit revealed in Christ is the true *subject* of our being. Christian faith therefore offers the experience of the one's identity in terms of oneness with the divine Spirit through Christ. "He who is joined to the Lord is one Spirit with him" (I Cor. 6:17). Out of this transforming experience of oneness the mystics said: I am a spark of the divine Light (Meister Eckhart), a drop of the divine ocean (Theresa of Avila), a flame of the divine fire (John of the Cross). I am a branch of the divine vine-stock (John 15:5), I am a fountain of the divine waters (John 7:38), I am a true son/daughter of God (Rom. 8:16), I am an heir of God, co-heir with Christ. (Rom. 8:17); God gives birth to himself in me (Origen), I am the mother God (Gregory of Nyssa), I give birth to the One who gives birth to me (Meister Eckhart).

This realisation of one's self-identity in terms of oneness with the divine Ground is not just a matter of the mental process. Mind can comprehend something, even our relationship with God, only in the framework of subject-object polarity. It is in the buddhi that one wakes up to the consciousness of union with the Divine and the resultant unity of reality. Entry into the *inner divine space* is however a gift of divine grace. The human seeker can through his discipline and asceticism control the mental activities and to some extent the movements in the psyche (*chittavrittis*). But access to the realm of inner light can be given only from within, from the divine Ground. "The Atman cannot be attained by instruction, nor through mental pursuits, not even through much hearing; he is to be attained only by the one whom the Atman chooses; to such a one the Atman reveals his nature" (Kath. Up. 2.23). The inner eye can be opened only by the divine Lord residing within; the inner light can be kindled only through the divine Flame. Hence the divine indwelling Master tells the human seeker: "Through your natural eye, you cannot see me; I give you a divine eye, now look!" (Bhag. Gita, 11,7). In Christian tradition too the role of divine grace is emphasised in the attainment of mystical union. "The depth of God can be known only by the Spirit of God" (I Cor. 2:10). This Spirit has been given to us, the Spirit that prays from within our hearts (Rom. 8:15,26). Only when the Spirit kindles buddhi, when the heart is filled with divine love, can one attain God. "God can be seen only in God's Light" (Thomas Aquinas). Human consciousness is transformed, deepened and integrated with the divine consciousness. The Divine in the human wakes up; the Divine unfolds itself through the human.

(For a diagram on the inward journey, see appendix p. 113)

3

THE INNER JOURNEY OF JESUS

What has been Jesus' inner spiritual journey? How did he go into the deeper levels of consciousness? It has been often narrated by the evangelists that Jesus used to retire to the solitude of the mountain to pray, to the silence of the night to commune with the Father. (Lk. 5:16, 6:12, 9:18,28, 11:1, 22:41). Jesus must have constantly asked himself at the buddhi level: who am I? Sinking into intense contemplative silence he experienced the deep oneness with the divine source, from which he perceived the salvific meaning of his mission. Jesus experienced the utter transparency of the human to the Divine within himself, the unfolding of the Divine through the human and the consequent divine mission. Hence he could say on the first step to his public ministry: "The Spirit of the Lord is upon me, for he has sent me forth to bring Good News to the poor..." (Lk. 4:18).

This has been a transforming process which involved much suffering. From the human side this meant surrender of the human ego to the divine Self. "During his life on earth, he offered up prayer and entreaty, with loud cries and with tears, to Him who had the power to save him from death, and he was heard because of his godly fear. Though he was Son, he learnt obedience through sufferings." (Heb. 5:7). The agony in Gethsemane (Mt. 26:36-39) and on the cross (Mt. 27:46) have been moments of intense suffering. And from the divine side this meant self-emptying (*kenosis*). "Though being in the form of God, he did not count equality with God as something to be grasped; but he emptied himself, taking the form of a slave, becoming as human beings are; and being in every way like a human being, he humbled himself, even to accepting death, death on a cross." (Phil. 2:6-8).

This inner journey was also a process of intense spiritual bliss. 'Rejoicing in the Spirit' Jesus communicated the Word of the Father to people. He lived and spoke out of an abiding consciousness that the Father was *with* him, *within* him. (John 8:16, 16:32, 14:10). He had the joy of doing what pleases the Father. (John 8:29, 10:11, 4:34, 5:17) The transfiguration on the mount must have been a dense expression of the ecstatic joy Jesus experienced in being one with the Father. (Lk. 9:29).

It is in the Gospel according to John that the inner spiritual experience of Jesus has been clearly described. Being a mystic himself, John sensed the depth of the mystical experience of Jesus. And being the beloved disciple, John had the privilege of being closer to the interior life and struggles of the divine Master. (John 13:23, 19:26). In the deep moments of ecstasy (Transfiguration on the mount) and in the intense moments of agony (Gethsemane, Calvary) John stood close to Jesus. While retiring to places of solitude Jesus must have often taken John with him. (John 1:39, Lk.9:28). John could then watch closely how the Master sank into deep contemplative silence and communed with the divine source of his life. Jesus must have shared with John some of his deepest spiritual experiences. (John 21:22,25). Perhaps no one knew Jesus so closely as John 'the disciple whom he loved' (John 13,23, 20:2, 21:7,20). This seems to explain why John could describe the inner search and struggles of Jesus as well as the intense experiences of Jesus' being one with the Father.

The Inner Experience of Jesus

In the God-consciousness of Jesus expressed in terms of Son-Father relation three dimensions can be noticed:

(i) 'The Father sent me' (3:17, 4:34, 5:36-38, 7:28-29, 10:36, 17:3). Jesus had an abiding consciousness of being sent by the Father. Here the Father is the one who sends the Son with the redemptive mission. The Son understands his mission as 'doing the will of the Father' (4:34, 5:30, 6:38), as 'completing the work of the Father' (4:34; 6:29; 9:3, 5:19, 10:37, 17:4). What is perceived here is a certain differentiation between the one who sends and the one who is sent. The relation between the Father and the Son is an *inter*-personal relation.

(ii)   'I am in the Father and the Father is in me' (5:26, 8:28, 14:10-20; 17:21,23). Jesus knew that the Father who sent him is with him, in him. (8:16,29, 16:32, 14:10). Here the Father is the one who gives life to the Son from within. The Son constantly takes birth from the Father (5:26; 6:57; 8:42; 16:28). The Father is the source and *generator* of the Son. Between them there is total mutual immanence, intense compenetration (*perichoresis*). The Son is the expression and unfolding of the Father (14:10; 12:49). There is no Father without the Son, no Son without the Father. The relation between the Father and the Son is an *intra*-personal relation.

(iii)   'The Father and I are One' (10:30: 17:11,21,22.) This is the articulation of the deepest experience of Jesus in relation to the Divine. He had the consciousness that his being and life and work have been totally transparent to the divine source, which he called the Father. (14:19) Father and Son are essentially one. The being of the Father reveals itself through the being of the Son. The Son is the self-communication of the Father. There is absolute unity between them. The relation between the Father and the Son is a *trans*-personal relation, in the sense that it goes far beyond the personalist structures of the human mind. The oneness in the depth of the Divine cannot be expressed in personalist categories.

These three aspects of Jesus' consciousness may not to be taken as three phases or spheres, but as the three integral dimensions of his God consciousness.

The inner experience of Jesus is a great mystery. Several theological attempts have been made to probe into this salvific mystery, mostly within the Greco-Roman forms of thinking. The mystical paradigm of Indian Vedanta could also be a help in continuing this search. The vedantic sages speak of three dimensions of God-consciousness:

(i)   I and the Divine are two. Here the emphasis is laid on the difference. The human and the Divine are experienced as two realities. This is the experience of duality (*dwaita*)

(ii)   I am a particle of the Divine. Here the emphasis is on participation, on the indwelling presence. The human is the abode of the Divine, part of the Divine. This is the experience of qualified-nonduality (*visishtadwaita*).

(iii)   I am one with the Divine. Here the emphasis is on unity, on One-ness. The human is totally one with the Divine. In fact there is no reality second to the Divine (*adwaita*).

All the three are integral dimensions of any genuine God experience: one cannot be isolated from the other. These may also be taken as phases in everyone's search for the Divine. This mystical triad need not be taken as a tool to interpret the experience of Jesus. In fact no mystical experience can be adequately interpreted with an external paradigm. However this vedantic perception could be a help to grasp the deeper dimensions of the inner experience of Jesus. In the inner journey of Jesus all the three dimensions can be found: he experienced his mission as being *sent* by the Father, his life *within* the Father and his being *one* with the Father.

The Abba Experience

Though in the Gospel the symbol *Father* is used within the limitations of the semitic language and patriarchal culture of the times, one could ask if this symbol has a deeper spiritual meaning and hence revelatory significance. It has been rightly pointed out that the use of the symbol *Father* by Jesus does have a certain uniqueness : Jesus spoke of God as 'my Father' with a deep intimacy (2:16; 3:35; 5:18; 6:32; 8:19; 15·9). While addressing God Jesus used the vocative form *Father* without any qualification. (17:1,5,11,21,24,25; Mt. 11:25; Mk.14:36; Lk.10:21; 23 :34,46). The term *Abo* in his mother tongue Aramaic actually means papa, daddy - forms which children often use to call their father in an affectionate way. Jesus was not merely speaking about God the Father, but revealing his deepest intimacy with God whom he called Father. This is something that transcends the semitic cultural psyche. Hence it is important that we go beyond the limitations of the cultural factors and explore the mystical significance of Jesus' experience.

At the time of Jesus the Jews did have forms of prayer addressed to God as Father. Hence there has been nothing objectionable in Jesus' use of this term. Yet, it is said, that they picked up stones to throw at him when he spoke of God as his Father (8:59; 10:31). They seemed to have sensed blasphemy in his use of the term Father while speaking of God or speaking to God. 'He spoke of God as his own Father, and so made himself God's equal!' (5:18) A reflection on Jesus' invocation form would therefore demand that we go beyond the format of the patriarchal culture and explore the mystical meaning of Jesus' language. The God-consciousness of Jesus cannot just be explained in terms of the semitic psyche, however important it is. What is decisive is not so much the name as the experience.

Indian sages constantly demand that the true seekers in pursuit of the Divine should incessantly go beyond the realm of names and forms *(nama-roopa)*. This holds good in interpreting a concrete experience of divine revelation too. No categorical symbol can exhaustively express the transcendent mystery of the Divine. Hence every name and form, every religious symbol, is fragmentary in relation to the unfathomable mystery that eludes it. Search for God experience cannot get stagnated in the experiences of the past or get fixated on certain names and forms. It is rather an inner pilgrimage, a relentless quest and unending pursuit *(sadhana)*, which alone would take the seeker into the inner recess of the mystery of reality. One has to carve deeper than the mental level and reach the light-sphere of buddhi. (Mund. Up. 3.1.5). In the divine Light one becomes light (Chand.Up. 4.5.3).

Father and Mother

There are two primordial symbols to speak about the Divine in terms of a personal relation : father and mother. In most of the primal religions both the symbols are profusely used. In the semitic religions there is a dominance of the use of the symbol *father*, while in the Indian religions the *mother* symbol plays a significant role in speaking of God. Jesus belonged to the semitc spiritual hemisphere and hence his language has been considerably conditioned by the historical and cultural factors of his country. Therefore it is not surprising that Jesus never addressed God as *mother*. Does it therefore mean that the motherly dimension of God-experience has been lacking in his consciousness? Is language merely a product of the cultural psyche? The Indian masters speak of an implied meaning of words (*dhwani*), especially in the poetic and mystical language. The density of spiritual experience can be perceived at this deeper level, not so much within the semantics of the language. Is it not then possible to dive below the surface of language in order to discover the deeper dimensions of Jesus' experience of the Divine? Such a search would demand that one reflects on the mystical symbols which Jesus consistently used to describe his experience of the Divine. A meditative entry into the inner world of Jesus with these symbols would reveal that the father-related language of Jesus evolved out of a mother-related experience of the Divine.

Since the archetypal symbols of father and mother are taken from the lived experience of human persons it may be good to explore their meaning in the context of the primal encounters in life. Observe a little child sitting on the lap of its father and leaning fondly on the chest of the father. The body contact with the father evokes a certain emotional response in the child. The child feels the protecting and supporting power of the father in whose hands he/she experiences security. In the father the child meets the other, the *thou,* and hence the relation with the father is an *inter*personal one: the father is greater than me. It is in meeting the father that the child makes the primal experience of encountering the other. For the child the father is the great *thou*. The Father is always above the child inviting it to grow, challenging, demanding and thus consolidating the individuality of the child.

Now look at the same child lying on the lap of his/her mother and being fed by the milk of the mother's breast. This is an intense body contact because of the flow of the vital sap from the mother's body into the mouth of the child. The child feels a deep oneness with the mother. For the child the mother is the primal *I*, and hence the relation is an *intra*personal one: I am in the mother and the mother is in me; I draw life from the mother and live through her. It is in feeling the mother that the child makes the pristine experience of being oneself. The child feels the mother not as someone else, but as the womb of its being, the source of life. In relation to the mother the child develops self-confidence.

This integral experience of the child in relation to his/her father and mother may help us to grasp the mystery of Jesus' relation with the Divine. Jesus experienced God as Father-and-Mother: as *thou* in an inter-personal mode and as the true *I* (Self) in an intra-personal way. In the words, 'the Fathers is greater than I', 'the Father sent me forth', 'It is my father's will..', 'I do what the Father has told me to do' etc. an I-thou relation with the Divine is evident (5:36; 6:40; 14:28,31). Here Jesus experiences God as the Father in an *inter* personal way. When on the other hand Jesus says, 'I am in my Father and the Father is in me', 'I come from within the Father', 'I draw life from the Father' (14:10; 17:21; 16:28; 8:42; 6:57) an *intra*personal I-Self relation with the Divine unfolds. In the latter frame Jesus experiences God as the Mother, the womb of his being, the ground of being and the motherly source of life. His *inter*personal relation with the Father reaches through the *intra*personal experience of the mother-dimension unto the *trans*personal oneness with the Divine: 'I and the Father are One' (10:30). And from within the trans-personal oneness with the Divine Jesus experienced the intra-personal motherliness of the Divine and expressed it in inter-personal categories referring to the Father. Deep within himself Jesus experienced the Divine as the *Mother*, though this experience has been articulated through the culturally conditioned symbol of the *Father*. Without paying attention to Jesus' experience of oneness with the Divine - and the consequent mother dimension - we cannot really speak of him as the Son of God. Jesus is Son of God not in the sense of Israel's kings or like 'all who are guided by the Spirit' (Rom. 8:14), but in the sense of being of the same nature of the Father (*homoousios*). He is Son not by adoption or vocation but by nature in eternal preexistence. This inner-trinitarian oneness can be adequately expressed only if the dimension of Jesus' experience of the Divine as *Mother* is taken seriously. The God in Jesus' consciousness is fatherly Mother and motherly Father at the same time, power and person, within him and beyond him, immanent and transcendent, *one* with him and at the same time *greater* than him.

When Jesus addressed God as Abba with a deep intimacy, he was not just using a male category of the contemporary patriarchal culture. Though the linguistic form connotes a father figure, the underlying experience is pregnant with mother-sentiments. Though the invocation is in a masculine form, the resonance comes from female vibrations. Though the term *Father* has masculine overtones, the way it is addressed has feminine undertones. When we are sensitive to the motherly dimension of his divine *consciousness*, we realize that Jesus was not in fact addressing a Father seated above him, but turning to the divine Mother dwelling within him. This is not just a question of shifting the gender language, but an invitation to dive into the mystical depth of the experience of Jesus. The Aramaic expression *Abbo, Abbi*, means the primal generating source of life: a = the primal; bb = life breath. [1] Jesus experienced the Divine as the source of his life and being; he addressed God as the ground of being, he called God as Father in the sense of the mother base, the womb of his being, the that-out-of-which (*yatah*) he came forth. This becomes clear when we meditate on some of the symbols Jesus used to describe his inner experience.

Symbols of Motherliness

In the mystical Gospel according to John the inner journey of Jesus has been described with symbols. Poetic symbols are in fact a more suitable medium to express mystical experience than mental concepts. Poetry is a better language of spirituality than dogma and philosophy. The fourth Gospel is rich in poetic images; most of them are archetypal symbols. Much of the classical Indian

---

[1] Douglas-Klotz, Neil, Prayers of the Cosmos, Meditations on the Aramaic Words of Jesus, Harper, San Francisco, 1990, 13.

Scriptures is poetry. The poets and sages of Asia chanted hymns to the glory of the all pervading divine presence. John's Gospel is often looked upon as a *Christopanishad*, a book of the wisdom on Jesus Christ written in poetry.

Five symbols are taken up here for a meditative reflection:

(i) **The Tree**. Jesus spoke of himself as the vinestock (15:5). No vinestock or stem of a tree stands by itself; it is supported and enlivened by the roots hidden in the mother earth. In the language of the stem Jesus said: 'I draw life from the Father', 'I am sent forth by the Father', 'I am in the Father, and the Father is in me' (6:57; 5:38; 14,10). The root which is the source of life has made the stem also the source of life (5:26). Just as the stem experiences the life-giving root Jesus experienced the Father. The root hidden in the womb of the mother earth is an archetypal symbol of the motherliness of the Divine. In this sense Jesus could say, that he 'came forth from the Father' (8:42; 13:3), and that he was 'sent forth by the Father' (7:29). "From him I am" (*par autou eimi*, 7:29) – this is a clear statement about the consciousness of consubstantiality between the Father and the Son (*homousios*). The root and the stem are in fact consubstantial. They are one, yet two: distinct but not separate. What binds them in unity is the constant flow of the vital sap. What makes the root give birth to the stem is the sap of the tree. This is the symbol of the Holy Spirit. Spirit is living water. (Mk. 1:10). Water is an archetypal symbol of the Spirit. (Is. 58:11; Jer. 2:13; Ez. 36:25). Like the life-giving fluid of the tree the Spirit flows from the Father to the Son and through the Son to the Father (*perichoresis*). The Spirit makes the Father give birth to the Son. Spirit is the power of life, stream of love within the Divine.

> Jesus experienced himself as the outgrowth of the divine stem (Son) into the world, born of the divine root (Father) and nourished by the divine sap (Spirit).

(ii) **The Well**. Jesus described himself as a well that offers the waters of divine life(4:14; 7:38). A well is the outpouring of the springs hidden in the mother earth. Jesus could offer 'streams of living water, the Spirit' (7:37-39) because he lived in the consciousness that in and through him the divine springs have been opened: 'I come forth from the Father', 'The Father who is the source of life has made the Son the source of life' (8:14,42; 5:26). Jesus experienced therefore the Divine as the hidden springs within himself: the Father is the self-outpouring motherly spring, the Son is the well that opens the spring. The Spirit is the flow of the water of divine life (3:5; 7:39; Rom. 5:5). What makes the hidden springs give birth to the well or river is the power immanent in the current. Spirit is the power within the Divine (*dynamis tou theou*, Acts 10:38). What comes forth from the hidden springs of the Father through the well, that the Son symbolizes, is the divne Spirit. Hence Jesus could invite all who are thirsty: "Come and drink from me!" (7:39). In this archetypal imagery too the outpouring of the hidden springs is the symbol of the motherliness of the Divine.

> Jesus experienced himself as the outflow of the divine well (Son),
> that opens the hidden divine springs (Father) and communicates
> the divine waters (Spirit).

(iii) **The Word**. The Gospel according to John begins with the hymn of Logos. Jesus is presented as the enfleshment of the 'Word that is God': Word *of* God and *with* God, Word *in* God and *out of* God.(1:1-5). Every word emerges out of the womb of silence. Father is eternal silence: 'No one has ever heard his voice' (5:37; 8:38). Son is the Word that unfolds the divine silence. [2] Jesus spoke with an abiding consciousness of being the voice of the Father. 'What I speak comes not from myself, but from within the Father' (3:34; 8:28;12:49; 14:10,24; 7:16). The Father is the true Self that speaks through the Son. The Father is the silence behind the Word that is born out of it. The words of Jesus came from within a deep sense of divine silence in the mystery of the Father. What fills the silence and the Word is the meaning, the content, the truth. Spirit is Truth: the Spirit *of* Truth, the Spirit *that is* Truth (14:17; 15:26). Spirit is the

---

[2] "Out of the eternal silence God spoke his Word" Ignatius of Antioch, Commentary to the Letter to the Ephesians, 19:1.

Truth of the Divine Word (16:13). What the Son communicates from within the Father is the divine Truth, that is the Spirit. The literal meaning of *truth* (*alletheia*) is opening, uncovering, unfolding. The Spirit unfolds the mystery of the Divine. Spirit is the immanent power that makes the Father generate the Son. "The Spirit explores the depths of everything, even the depths of God." (I Cor. 2:10) Our response should be 'worshipping God in Spirit and Truth' (4:23-24).

> Jesus experienced himself the expression of the divine Word (Son) that articulates the divine silence (Father) and communicates the divine Truth (Spirit).

(iv) **The Feeding Breast**. The Prologue of the Gospel ends with an impressive imagery; the Son is clinging on to the feeding breast of the Father (1:18). The Greek word *kolpos* has often been translated as bosom or heart. But its primary meaning is the feeding breast of the mother. The Greek preposition *eis* connotes a movement towards something, a movement of adherence, a clinging on to someone. Hence the expression *eis ton kolpon* offers the image of a child clinging on to the feeding breast of its mother. 'No one has ever seen God except the only begotten Son who clings on to the feeding breast of the (divine motherly) Father'. Here the relationship of the divine Son to the Father is that of a child to its mother.

> Jesus understood himself as the child (Son) that is being fed by the divine mother (Father) with the sap of divine life (Spirit).

(v) **The Fountain:** With the experience of the Divine as Mother, Jesus understood himself as the unfolding of the divine motherly source : as the well (Son) that opens the springs (Father) and pours out the water (Spirit). 'The Father who is the source of life has made the Son the source of life'(5:26). Hence Jesus could ecstatically invite people to the divine well opened in him: 'come and drink from me' (7:37-38; 4:14). Who can say this except a mother to her child? Just as the milk from the mother's body becomes the vital sap in the child, the living water that one drinks from Christ becomes 'a spring welling up to eternal life' in the believer (4:14; 7:38).[3]

> Jesus presented himself as the embodiment of the divine compassion (Son) that emerges from the divine motherliness (Father) and communicates the life-giving divine tenderness (Spirit).

God as the Subject

If Jesus experienced the Divine as *Mother*, it was the experience of the Divine as the true *subject* of his being. The term subject has to be understood here in the proper mystical sense. It does not mean to deny the human soul of Jesus, nor does it negate the inner-trinitarian distinction between the Father and the Son. It rather emphasizes the life-giving relation of the Father to the Son within the divine reality. Jesus experienced the Father as the *whence* of his being (*yatah*): the birthing ground and motherly source, the inner springs and nourishing root. In this sense the Father is the ultimate source of the life and work of the Son. The Father is the *subject* of the Son, made manifest in Jesus. It is with this subject-consciousness that Jesus could say:

> My teaching is not from myself; it comes from the one who sent me (7:16).
> What I say, is what the Father has taught me (8:28).
> What I say to you, I do not speak of my own accord: it is the Father living in me is doing his works (14:10).
> The word that you hear is not my own: it is the word of the Father who sent me (14:24).
> I have not spoken of my own accord; but the Father who sent me commanded me what to say and what to speak; what the Father has told me is what I speak. (12:49-50).
> He whom God has sent speaks God's own words (3:34).
> I passed your word on to them (17:14).
> I act just as the Father commanded (14:31).

---

[3] The creed of the Council of Toledo (675) has a significant phrase: *Filius natus vel genitus est de utero Patris* (the Son is born or generated from within the womb of the Father). In the Middle Ages there has been in the Church a trend of devotion to Jesus the Mother.

I perform the works of my Father (5:36).
I have come to do the will of him who sent me (6:38)

These and similar sayings of Jesus reveal that the Father is the *whence* of the Son, the true subject of Jesus. In the deepest subject-consciousness Jesus could exclaim: The Father and I are one (10:30). The awareness of this oneness is at work in all the works and words of Jesus. A discovery of this depth dimension is vital in understanding the *mysterium Christi.*

The Asian spiritual perception is basically one of deep mystical oneness. Overwhelmed by the universal immanence of the Divine the sages describe reality in terms of its ultimate unity within the Divine. Both the duality (*dwaita*) and participation (*visishtadwaita*) perceptions are nourished by the undercurrent of an awareness of deep one-ness (*adwaita*). The sage who intuits the ontic oneness experiences the Divine as the ultimate subject of reality:

"He is the unseen seer, the unheard hearer, the unthought thinker, the unknown knower. There is no other seer than he, no other hearer than he, no other thinker than he, no other knower than he. He is your atman, the inner controller, the immortal Self" (Brh. Up. 3,7,23). How to know the true knower within us? (*vijnataram kena vijaneeyat,* Brih.Up. 4.5.15) – this is the basic quest of the Indian sages. This is the relentless mystical quest for the divine subject within us. In a moment of grace one may exclaim: I am divine! (*aham brahmasmi.* Brih. Up. 1.4.10).

This does not mean that the individuality of the person or the reality of the world is denied; rather one intuits the ultimate source of being and life. At the level of the mental perception one sees diversity; but at the level of the intuitive buddhi one experiences the ultimate unity of reality. Mind objectifies everything including God, but the buddhi intuits the Divine as the ultimate *subject.* As the subject of all, the divine Spirit permeates everything and operates through everything. The entire universe is a theophany, for 'everything is enveloped by the Divine' (*isavasyamidam sarvam,* Isa Up.1). The deeper mystical meaning of the *I am* sayings of Jesus can be grasped only at the level of the buddhi.

The Triune God

Meditation on these mystical symbols of Jesus's inner experience throws some light on the mystery of the Divine as Trinity. Before any reflection on the Trinity is made it must be affirmed that we dare to speak on a reality on which we should actually keep silence. The early Fathers of the Church were very conscious of the human *aporie* when reflecting on the mystery of the Divine. They knew that "human words would only hide God more than they reveal him" (Augustine). The reality of the Divine is ever beyond any human comprehension. No speculative endeavour can exhaustively articulate the divine reality. No particular revelatory experience can fully and exhaustively unfold the mystery of God. The warning of Augustine on every theological pursuit is ever valid: "If you understand God, it is not God". (*si comprehendisti, non est Deus!* PL. 8,663). The hermits of the Egyptian desert were so overwhelmed by this mystery that they often sank into contemplative silence. One of them, Theophilus (3. century), said: if you do not understand my silence, you cannot understand my words. Gregory of Nyssa used to tell the seekers: "It is not by knowing through concepts and images that you know God, but only by going into the inner darkness, by entering like Moses the cloud of the mountain." (Commentary on the Song of Songs). In the subsequent mystical traditions of the Church this sense of the mystery was constantly upheld. The God-seeker has to transcend the mind and go through the *cloud of the unknowing* (English mystic), the *dark night of the soul* (John of the Cross), in order to reach the inner source of divine light. This however is not just the light, as the mind would have it, but *effulgent darkness* (Dyonisius the Areopagite, Myst.Theol). It is by conjoining the opposites that the human mind may predicate something on to God: light and darkness, being and non-being, far and near, *coincidentia oppositorum* (Nicholas of Cusa). In short , "one has to become god-less in order to experience God, for God is God-beyond-God." (Meister Eckhart). Thomas Aquinas, who reflected so much on God, was clear on the basic truth: know that one does not know God. (*quod homo sciat se Deum nescire.* (*De Potentia*, 7.5. ad 14.)

The Upanishadic sages of ancient India too were very sensitive to the incomprehensibility of the divine mystery.

"There the eye does not reach, the speech does not go, nor the mind. We do not know it; we do not know how to teach it. It is other than the known, and beyond the unknown. It is not understood by those who understand it; it is rather understood by those who do not understand it." (Kena Up. 1.3.4; 2.3)

In all contemplative pursuits 'human words recoil along with the mind not attaining the Absolute'. (Tait.Up. 2.4) "The *atman* cannot be attained by instruction or by mental pursuits or through much hearing" (Mund.Up.. 3.2.3). Hence to every predicate we have on the divine mystery we must add: not so, not so (*neti, neti.* Brih, Up. 3.9.26). Perhaps the only language that would suit this would be that of conjoining the opposites: *Brahman* is being and non-being, far and near, light and darkness

In each of the symbols which we examined in Jesus' language three dimensions of the divine reality can be seen:

(i) The Father as Mystery. The root, well-spring and silence point to the aspect of hiddenness. There is no direct access to any of these. The symbol of the *Father* refers to the ineffable mystery of the Divine. Jesus experienced the Father primarily as the divine mystery within him. "The Father is greater than I" (14:28). In fact the root is deeper than the stem, the hidden springs are more than the outflow, the silence is richer than the words. No concrete self-expression of the Divine can give us a full access to the divine mystery. "No one has seen the Father; no one has heard his voice" (5:37). Even the reality of Christ eludes our full grasp. "You do not know where I come from" (8:14). The Father as the *whence* of the Son always remains an incomprehensible mystery for us. At the same time the Father is the symbol of the source of divine life. The Son is born from the *womb* of the Father (Ambrose). God as Father is the generating *mother-base* of the Divine. Jesus lived out of this consciousness of the Father: "I come out of the Father" (8:42; 16:28), "I draw life from the Father" (6:57).

(ii) The Son as the Word. The second element of the three symbols points to the self-unfolding of the Divine. The stem unfolds the hidden root, the well opens up the hidden springs, the word articulates the silence. The Son is the self-communication of the Father: the outgrowth of the divine root, the outpouring of the divine fountain, the articulation of the mystery of divine silence. The Son is the 'the image of the unseen God' (Col. 1:15), the language of the Divine, the *ekstasis tou theou*. Jesus lived out of this consciousness of being the Son of God.

> Anyone who sees me, sees the Father (14:9).
> Anyone who knows me, knows the Father (14:7).
> Anyone who hears me, hears the Father (14:10).
> Anyone who listens to me, listens to the Father (8:47).
> Anyone who believes in me, believes in the Father (12:44).
> Anyone who welcomes me, welcomes the Father (13:20).
> Anyone who hates me, hates the Father. (15:23).

In Jesus Christ we see with the eyes of faith the Word incarnate, the face of God turned towards humanity, the hand of God stretched out to embrace the estranged world. Jesus is *Emmanuel*, God-with-us here and now.

(iii) The Spirit as the Power. What is communicated through these three symbols is in fact the immanent power of life. Through the stem the vital sap is given from within the womb of the root; through the well / river the refreshing water is poured out from the springs; through the word the truth is articulated from the silence of the mind. Through the Son the divine Spirit is sent forth from the Father. It is in the Spirit that the Father generates the Son. Spirit permeates the Father and the Son as the immanent divine energy (*perichoresis*). Spirit explores the depth of the Divine (I Cor. 2:10). Spirit is the self-communication of the divine life (6:63), the self-manifestation of the divine light (8:12), the self-revelation of the divine truth (14:17), the self-outpouring of the divine love (Rom. 5:5). Jesus experienced himself as the channel of the divine Spirit. He was born of the Spirit (Lk. 1:35), brought up by the Spirit (Lk.1:80), filled with the Spirit (Lk. 4:1), anointed by the Spirit (Lk.4:18), led by the Spirit (Lk. 4:14), enlightened by the Spirit (Lk.10:21) and empowered by the Spirit (Mt. 12:28). Jesus lived out a deep consciousness of the Father as the subject of his being (14:10) and of the Spirit as the power within himself (Mt.12:28). In this sense Jesus Christ is the self-outpouring of the divine presence in the world. Hence he could say the inviting words: those who are thirsty, come and drink from me; out of the centre of your being shall flow streams of the divine Spirit. (7:37-39).

The Divine as Self-Communication

The inner journey of Jesus offers the light to look into the abysmal mystery of the Divine and realise the trinitarian process therein. In his light we see light. In his experience we experience the Divine. Other religions do have other ways of entering into the mystery of the Divine, and these must be respected as valid ways of God-experience. The ineffable mystery of the Divine manifests itself in diverse ways. God is within and beyond all religions. There is no last word on God, there is no absolute religion. Any experience of God is a groping experience. Any revelation of the divine mystery has a fragmentary character. When we look into the *depths of the Divine* in the light of the experience of Jesus, we realise that God is a self-giving reality. Divine life is a self-unfolding process: like the root unfolding itself through the stem, like the hidden springs pouring out as the stream, like the silence articulating itself in the word. These mystical symbols point to the truth: the trinitarian Divine is not a static reality, but a constant self-outpouring of life. God is not like a self-contained lake resting in itself on the mountaintop, but like a lake that continuously pours itself out into the river; but the lake continues to be lake for it is nourished by the hidden springs. God as Trinity means that God is Love: love is self-giving. God as Trinity means God is a Living God: life is a self-transcending process. In this process of the inner-trinitarian life three dimensions may be recognised: to be within itself, to go out of itself, to return to itself. Similarly in the process of the love too three dimensions are present: to be within myself, to go out of myself to the thou, and to return to me. In as much as one could discern *vestigium trinitatis* in the human experience of life and love one may speak of the Trinity as follows:

God-within-self (*enstasis*) – this is the Father
God-out-of-self (*ekstasis*)– this is the Son
God-unto-self (return) – this is the Spirit.
> Father is the *I*
> Son is the *Thou*
> Spirit is the *We*.

God above all – this is the Father
God through all – this is the Son
God in all – this is the Spirit (cfr. Eph. 4:6).
> Father is the beginningless beginning
> Son is the self-communication of God
> Spirit is the healing presence of God

Father is the Ground and Abyss of the Divine
Son is the freedom and love of the Divine
Spirit is the communion and relationality of the Divine.
> Father refers to the dimension of transcendence
> Son points to the dimension of immanence
> Spirit conveys the dimension of transparence.

The eternal Silence of the Divine – this is the Father
The eternal Word of the Divine – this is the Son
The eternal Wisdom of the Divine – this is the Spirit.

One does not come after the other; all the three dimensions are always one, yet three. These expressions are in fact a groping of the human mind in exploring the ineffable mystery of the Divine. Every predication has to be affirmed and denied, for the mystery of the Trinity continues to be incomprehensible.

Father, Son and Spirit are One, yet three: one in being (*homousios, consubstantial*) and yet there is a distinction of the three (*hypostaseis / prosopa /personae*). "Each in each, each in all, all in each, all in all, all in One." (Augustine, De Trinitate, 7.6.11). "One with one, one from one, one in one and One eternal." (Meister Eckhart, Vom edlen Menschen). "We hold the distinction, not the confusion of Father, Son and Holy Spirit: a distinction without separation, a distinction without plurality" (Ambrose, To Gratian, 4,8). The Trinitarian mystery reveals that God is not one-alone (*unus*), but One (*unum*), not *ekah* but *ekam*, not solitary but communion. The divine unity is triune. The use of the neutral in designating the oneness, shows that there is a dynamism within the One. The early theologians and councils spoke of *perichoresis* in order to point to this inner-trinitarian dynamism of life and love. *Father, Son and Spirit* may be understood as *symbols* pointing to this eternal divine process. Christian faith in God is not strictly *mono*theistic but *trini*tarian.

The Fathers of the Church were overwhelmed by the insight into the inner-trinitarian dynamics. Leaning on the symbolic language of John's Gospel they profusely used poetic symbols to speak of the mystery of the Trinity.

"God brought forth the Word
>   as the root brings forth the shoot,
>   as the spring brings forth the stream,
>   as the sun brings forth the beam of light.
Each of these manifestations is
an outflow of being from its respective source.
And I would not hesitate to say that
>   the shoot is the *son* of the root,
>   the stream is the *son* of the spring,
>   the beam of light is the *son* of the sun;
every source is a mother-base,
and everything that is brought forth from the source is its offspring.
>   Much more is true of the Word of God,
>   who received the name of the Son in the proper sense.
>   (Tertullian, Adversus Praxean, 8)

The Son is derived from the fountainhead of the Father.
>   (Origen, Comment. On John, 2.2.10)

The Son comes out of the Father
>   as light from light,
>   as water from a fountain,
>   as ray from the sun.   (Hyppolytus, MG. 10,817)

The Son is begotten from the *bowels* of the Father (*de utero patris*):
>   the Father is the fountain and root of the Son's being.
>   (Ambrose. ML. 16,642)

The Son is the Intelligence, Reason, Wisdom of the Father,
>   and the Spirit is the effulgence, as light from fire.
>   (Athenagoras MG. 6, 945)

The whole being of the Son is proper to the Father's essence,
    as radiance from light,
    as stream from fountain.
The Father is the Son, since the Son is
what is from the Father and proper to him:
    as the sun in the radiance,
    as the thought in the word,
    as the fountain in the stream.
They are *one,* not as one thing divided into two parts,
    not as one thing twice named.
They are two, because the Father is Father, not also Son,
    the Son is Son, not also Father.

(Athanasius, MG. 26,328)

The Spirit proceeds like fruit proceeding from the root through the bud.

(Tertullian, Adv. Praxean, 8)

Two insights seem to emerge from this poetic language:

(i) The *one* in the triune God does not mean a static unity, but a dynamic Oneness: God is a living God. God's being is Self-communication. God is love. In this sense God's being is *becoming.*

(ii) The *three* in the triune God does not refer to three persons in the sense of our present day understanding of person as an individual with an independent centre of freedom and will. Rather, the Trinity consists of a threefold *subsisting relation.*

In all these patristic meditations the divine Trinity is experienced as the dynamic source of life and love. And this source opened itself out into history through the person of Jesus Christ. Hence Peter could look at Jesus with the eyes of faith and exclaim: you are the Son of the living God.(Mt.16:16). Jesus understood himself as the self-outpouring of the divine fountains, as the self-revelation of the divine mystery, as the self-articulation of the divine silence; as the Son of the divine Father. Hence he could say:No one comes to the Father except through me (14:6).

Jesus lived and spoke out of a deep awareness of his oneness with the Father and transparency to the Spirit. He felt the presence of the Father like living fountain within himself and the power of the Spirit like a stream of life; and he experienced himself as the unfolding of the Father in the Spirit. The Father reveals himself through the Son and communicates the Spirit. Through Jesus the Christ the eternal Son embodied himself in history.

An Indian Meditation on the Trinity

That the Divine is an unfathomable mystery, that God is the ultimate fountain of life and love – this is a universal experience. In different religions sages contemplate this mystery in diverse ways. However a certain triadic structure can be noticed in the way several sages describe the inner-divine process of self-giving. The Upanishadic sage acknowledges this:

> This is a triadic structure (*trayam va idam*)
> The three together form the One (*tadetat trayam*)
> The atman is One,yet triadic (*atma ekah, sannekat trayam*)
> (Brih. Up. 1.6.1,3)

In the mystical experiences of Indian sages a certain perception of the mystery of the Trinity can be noticed:

The Divine as the ontic Ground of Truth *(satyam);*
The Divine as the consciousness unfolding the divine Ground *(jnanam);*
The Divine as infinity emerging out of the Ground (*anandam*) (Tait.Up. 2.1.1).

> God as the Truth of the ultimate being (*satyam*)
> God as the grace of the Divine (*sivam*)
> God as the beauty of the divine life (*sundaram*).

God as the primordial 'whence' (*yatah*)
God as the immanent 'through' (*yena*)
God as the ultimate 'whither' (*yam*) (Tait Up. 3,1).

> The Divine as unfathomable mystery (*Brahman*)
> God as the divine Lord (*Iswara*)
> Spirit as the divine immanence (*Atman*).

From the Fullness (*purnat*)
evolves the Fullness (*purnamudachyate*);
What remains is Fullness (*purnameva avasishyate*) (Upan. Santipadam).

> The experience of the Divine as utter Transcendence (*Nirguna*)
> The meeting with the Divine in names and forms (*Saguna*)
> The insertion into the field of divine power (*Sakti*).

The awareness of the divine mystery (*jnana*)
The encounter with the divine master (*bhakti*)
The creative response to the divine immanence (*karma*) (Bhag. Gita,12:6)[4]

In order to enter deep into the experience of the inner-divine life the sages propose the meditative repetition of the manthra "OM". The constitutive sounds of OM are A, U, and M. *A* is the very first sound one can produce; *M* is the closing humming sound; the middle sound is *U*. Hence *A* is the beginning, *U* is the middle and *M* is the end. All the three together form the manthra OM. (a + u = o). OM is therefore the sound symbol of the divine omnipresence. OM is the articulation of the divine vibration in the cosmos, the expression of the divine creativity, the syllable of the divine presence here and now. OM is the primal revelation of the divine mystery. (Chand. Up. 1.1.2; 2.23.3; Maitri Up. 6.22; Prasna Up. 5.5). Dwelling on this divine sound Swami Abhishiktananda (Dom Le Saux) offers an insightful meditation on the Trinity:

> OM that emerges from the Silence of the Father, opens up in its depths for the uttering of the Word, and concludes ineffably in the Spirit.

> OM that sings at once all the inner movement of God towards himself and also all his inner repose within himself.

> OM that speaks of the communication of the Fullness to the Son and the Spirit – and also to all those who in the Son accept this gift - and the return of the same Fullness to the Father.

> OM that, in this return to the Father, is identical with the *Abba Father*, which is eternally prayed by the Son and murmured ceaselessly by the Spirit in the hearts of all saints.

> OM is the dawn of Being in the Father (*sat*), OM is Being's self-awareness, its awakening to itself, in the Son (*chit*), OM is the

---

[4] For insightful reflections on an Indian understanding of the Trinity: Abhishiktananda, Saccidananda, A Christian Approach to Advaitic Experience, ISPCK, Delhi, 1974.

Von Brück, Michael, The Unity of Reality. God, God-Experience and Meditation in the Hindu-Christian Dialogue, Paulist Press, New York, 1986.

tremor at the ultimate threshold of sound, which is the Spirit in God and in the universe.

Each of the Three utters OM for oneself, and the Three utter it as One. Each one utters it in its entirety, for each celebrates the Three, and their indivisible unity as well.

I also sing OM. I utter OM, whose source is the Father, the OM which resounds in me and comes to silence in the Spirit. Indeed, I am this OM, which I utter, for I myself do not exist as a unique person except in the Logos, in the OM, in which creation came to be.

I am the OM, which the Father pronounces through the Son in the Spirit, God's infinite flight within himself towards himself.

I am *Sat-chit-ananda*, the very mystery of God, the truest expression of the Divine and at the same time the ultimate secret of mine too.[5]

---

[5] Abhishiktananda, Saccidananda, ISPCK, Delhi, 1974, 189-191

4

DIVINISATION OF THE HUMAN

Who am I? – this is the basic question that resounds in all genuine spiritual pursuits. On the inner journey of every seeker towards the divine centre this question consciously or unconsciously accompanies the seeker. The answer one receives – however fragmentary – gives light and courage in life. In all religions this question is articulated and the answers are offered in diverse ways. In spite of the differences in the perceptions one can discover converging lines in these answers.

In his inner journey Jesus went to the divine core of his life with this question. His experience is expressed in the mystical symbols, on which we meditated in the previous chapter. Jesus experienced himself as the Son of God, the Word of the divine silence, the stem that unfolds the divine root, the well that opens the divine springs. If this had been his experience, what did Jesus wish to communicate to his disciples, to us who believe in him as the way?

As in Jesus, so in us

Let us look at the symbol of the tree. The vital sap that flows from the root to the stem flows further upward into all the branches. *Just as* the stem is conjoined to the root, the branches are conjoined to the stem. *Just as* the stem grows out of the root, the branches grow out of the stem. Ultimately there is no difference between the relationship of the stem with the root and the relationship of the branches with the stem. But there is a difference among them! The root does not become the stem, nor do the branches turn into the stem. Yet they are one in reality. The one vital sap flows from the root through the stem into the branches. The entire tree is *one*!

With this archetypal imagery Jesus said: "I am the stem, you are the branches." Keeping this symbol in mind we could sense the deeper mystical meaning of the sayings of Jesus as found in the Gospel according to John:

> Just as the Father sent me into the world, so do I send you into the world (17:18).
> Just as the Father knows me, I know my own (10:15)
> Just as the Father has loved me, so have I loved you (15:9;17:26).
> Just as I remain in the love of the Father, so will you remain in my love (15:10).
> Just as I draw life from the Father, so will you draw life from me (6:57).
> Just as I am in the Father, and the Father is in me, so am I in you and you are in me (17:21;14:20).
> Just as the Father and I are one, so may you all be one in us (17:21-22).

The Greek preposition *kathos* (just as) has a great significance here. Jesus wanted that all those who believe in him make the same inner journey that he made, and participate in the same inner experience that shaped his consciousness.

We have seen above that there are basically three dimensions in the inner experience of Jesus: (i) The Father sent me, (ii) I am in the Father and the Father is in me, and (iii) the Father and I are one. (10:30). Correspondingly Jesus said:

> *Just as* the Father sent me, I send you (17:18)
> *Just as* the Father is in me, and I am in the Father, you are in me, and I am in you. (17:21; 14:20)
> *Just as* the Father and I are one, may you be one in us (17:21).

It is significant that Jesus spoke these words in the last discourse, a few moments before his *passover*. He wants us all to realise that we are sons/daughters of God: that we are all one within the inner-trinitarian life. It is the realisation that the divine presence that unfolded itself in Jesus continues the self-unfolding in us all. It is the awareness that the same divine Spirit that filled and moved Jesus fills and moves all those who wake up to the divine consciousness. It is the experience of the Spirit guiding our life

(Gal. 5:16) from within our heart, transforming us into the *new being* revealed in Jesus (Rom. 8:15). It is the enlightened consciousness that we are branches of the divine Tree (Jn 15:5), streams of the divine waters (Jn. 7:38), members of the body of Christ (I Cor. 12:12), heirs of God and coheirs of Christ (Rom. 8:17). All this means liberation from a superficial, ego-centered, consumerist self-identity to a deeper, God-centered, holistic self-realisation: liberation from 'life according to the flesh' (*sarkikos*) to 'life according to the Spirit' (*pneumatikos*) (Rom. 8:5-8; Gal. 5: 18-24). "Anyone who holds on to his life will lose it; anyone who loses his life for my sake will save it for eternal life." (Mk.8:35; Jn. 12:25). One has to be reborn to a deeper self-consciousness 'reborn in Spirit and water' (3:1). This is an invitation to a divine consciousness, to the discovery of one's true self-identity within the inner-trinitarian divine life-process. Our life unfolds not so much before God as within the Divine, *just as* the branches unfold from the root through the stem in the flow of the vital sap. Our spiritual life evolves from the Father through the Son in the Spirit. We are called to 'share the divine nature' (II Pet.1:4). The question, *who am I*, needs to be put in this process.

In this deeper Christic consciousness, which is a grace, we realise the transformation that is going on in the *divine space* within us. The divine Spirit transforms our life into the divine life, integrates our life with the inner-trinitarian process. The divine sap (the Spirit) that flows from the root (the Father) through the stem (the Son) enlivens all the branches and leaves, i.e. all who are inserted to the stem. Our life merges with the divine life; our being is rooted on the divine Ground; our existence is enlivened by the hidden divine springs. Mystics try to describe this experience with poetic imageries: our true self is like waves of the divine ocean, like sparks of the divine fire, like beams of the divine sun, like branches of the divine tree. Who am I? *I am divine!*

Symbols of Christ-in-us

Jesus presented himself as the *way* to the process of this realization. He awakens in us the divine consciousness that unfolded in him.

In and through him we become one with the Divine. Our relationship to Christ has to grow deeper than the mere I-thou relationship. Our life unfolds *in Christo*. This becomes clear when we meditate on the Christ-symbols associated with the *I am* statements of Jesus of the Gospel according to John. These are not just objectifying symbols, but assimilative symbols:

> I am the bread of life (6:35, 48). Bread is not an object to be kept on the table, but something to be eaten and assimilated.
>
> I am the living water (4:14) Water is not just to be preserved in a bottle, but to drink.
>
> I am the light (8:12) . We do not see light as an object, rather we see everything in the light.
>
> I am the way, the door (14:6, 10:7). The way is for us to go along, the door is to pass through.
>
> I am the life (14:6). Life is not something apart from us, life is what we truly are.
>
> I am the truth (14:6). Truth is not something that remains outside, but that which opens (*alletheia*) our mind.
>
> I am the good shepherd (10:11). The good shepherd is not the one who stands apart, but the one who lets his life merge into that of the sheep.
>
> I am the vinestock (15:5). The vinestock is not an object separated from the branches, but the source and subject of their life.

With these symbols Jesus tries to make clear who he is for us, and how our relation to him in faith evolves. Jesus Christ is not just a person of the historical past, but the divine presence here and now. Christ is *Emmanuel*: God with us, God within us. He cannot just be looked upon as a being apart from us: we are in him, he is in us. He is the stem through which we live in God, he is the well from which we are *spirit*ually nourished, he is the light in which we see everything, he is divine life by which we live.

Christic Consciousness

Paul consistently emphasises this mystical dimension of our relationship with Christ: Everyone who is joined to the Lord is one Spirit with him (I Cor. 6:17). Our true life merges with the life of Christ in us. Faith is insertion to divine life through Christ. In faith we recognize:

our life is hidden in Christ.(Col.3:3),
we are reborn in Christ (II Cor.5:17),
we grow into maturity in Christ (Eph. 3: 16),
we are clothed in Christ (Gal. 3:27),
we are being transformed into the image of Christ (II Cor. 3:18),
we reflect the glory of Christ (II Cor. 3:18)
we live the life of Christ (Gal. 2:20)
we mature into the fullness of Christ (Eph. 4:13)
we are being renewed in Christ (Gal.6:15)
Christ is in us (Rom.8:10)
we are in Christ (Eph. 1:4)
Christ is our life (Phil. 1:20, Rom. 6:23)
Christ is our light (II Cor. 4:6)
Christ is our freedom (II Cor.3:17, Gal. 5:1, Rom. 8:2)
we are the heirs of God, co-heirs of Christ (Rom.8:17)
we are the limbs of the body of Christ (I Cor. 12:27)
Christ is the fulfilment of our life (Col. 2:10)

In the deepest experience of this Christic consciousness we should be able to cry out with Paul: I live, not I, Christ lives in me (Gal.2:20). To believe in Christ means not just relating us to Jesus as the historical person of the past, but inserting us to the present reality of the living Christ. Christ is God with us, God within us, God all-in-all. The Letter to the Ephesians describes unto what experience this Christic consciousness finally leads us: to be filled with the utter fullness of God (3:19).

Such expressions cannot just be grasped by human efforts, nor can they be fully understood through the reasoning process of the discursive mind. The mystics demand that we go deeper than the mental operations and open ourselves to the intuitive movements in the buddhi. This however is a gift of grace. When we are graced with this en*light*enment, we realise the divine core of our being, the divine dimension of our true self within. Then we may be able to exclaim: *we are divine*!

The Process of Divinisation
The early Fathers of the Church and the mystics of later centuries had deep insights into the spiritual undercurrents of our life-

process.[1] They spoke clearly about the divinisation of the human (*theosis*). (the use of the term *man* has to be taken here in the gender-inclusive sense)

> "God became man so that man may become God!" (*Deus homo factus est, ut homo fieret Deus*, Augustine, PL.38,1997).

> "Through his immense love the Word of God became what we are, so that we may become perfectly what he is." (Iraeneus PG. 7,1120)

> "This is why the Word became man, and the Son of God became Son of man: so that man, by entering into communion with the Logos and thus receiving the divine sonship, might become a son of God." (Iraeneus, PG. 25,192 b)

> "When our consciousness is completely purified and through contemplation elevated above the material realm, it will be divinised by God." (Origen,Comm. on John 32,17, PG. 14. 817a)

> "With Jesus human and divine nature begin to be woven together so that by fellowship with divinity human nature might become divine, not only in Jesus, but also in all those who believe, and go on to undertake the life which Jesus taught."(Origen,Contra Celsum, 3,28)

> "The Word became man, so that we humans may become Divine." (Athanasius, PG. 25,192)

> "Theosis means the re-forming of the Image of God according to which we have been created by the Word, the restoration of the knowledge of God through the knowledge that came in the humanity of the Logos." (Athanasius De Incarnatione 3,101; 13,120)

> "There is a divine seed in man: man becomes not God, but is being divinised." (Clement of Alexandria, Stromata, 7,10,57)

> "In the Spirit the Word divinises us." (Athanasius, PG.25, 192; 26,589)

> "In the Holy Spirit the divine Word divinises us." (Origen, PG. 26,589)

> "Christ takes shape in us through the Holy Spirit who reinstates the divinity in us." (Cyril of Alexandria, PG.75,1088)

---

[1] Myrraha Lot-Borodine, La Deífication de L'homme selon la doctrine des Peres grecs, Editions du Cerf, Paris, 1970.

Edmund J. Fortman SJ, The Theolgoy of Man and Grace, Readings in the Theology of Grace, Bruce, Milwaukee, 1966, 81-148.

"Christ is Son by nature, we are sons by grace." (Athanasius, PG 26,361c)

"We have not only become Christians, but Christ himself. Stand firm in awe and rejoice: we have become Christ." (Augustine, Commentary on John's Gospel, 21,8)

"Theosis is participation through grace in that which surrounds the nature of God." (John of Damascus, Expositio Fidei, 88,18).

"Theosis is exaltation of nature, not its destruction." (Athanasios of Sinai, Viae Dux, 2,7,,8)

"Through theosis we are brought into the energy-field of God." (Gregorios Palamas, Holy Hesychasts).

"The only begotten Son of God, wanting to make us sharers in his divinity, assumed our nature, so that he, made man, might make men gods." (Thomas Aquinas, Opus 57, 1-4)

Divinisation means the reinstatement of the image of God fully in us. What humanity had lost through the *Fall* has been reinstated through the salvific event of Jesus Christ. The clouds which hide our true nature are being removed by the light of the risen Christ in us. In the power and presence of the Holy Spirit we recognize who we truly are. The Spirit makes us realise that we are no more slaves but sons and daughters of God, participating in the divine nature through Christ. The Fathers of the Church do not equate human soul with the pre-existent divine Son, but they emphasise that through the Incarnation of the Logos the Divine that is dormant in us is awakened in Jesus; through Christ we have been graced with the realisation that we participate in the new humanity that is one with the divinity of Christ. We are grafted onto the tree of Christ (Rom. 11:17). Christ is God-within-us here and now. We are called to be partners with Christ (I Cor.1:9), shares of divine life (I Jn 1:3, II Peter. 1:4). So we put on the new Man (Col. 3:10), and become a new creation (II Cor. 5:17). We live *in Christ*. Christ lives through us.

Giving Birth to God

This is a *birthing* process : God gave birth to us; we give birth to God. Several Fathers of the Church use the imagery of the *birth of God in the soul*. We are all called to become not only children of God, but also mothers of God. "What once happened in a bodily way in the virgin Mary continues to happen in every human soul that is totally open to God : to become mother of God."(Gregory of Nyssa, Comm. on Mathew, 12,50) "When God works in the soul, the soul receives the Word and becomes pregnant in the Spirit. Thus the soul becomes like a mother giving birth to God."(Origen, Comm. on Song of Songs). Reflecting on what happened in Bethlehem Augustine preached : "Christ is born; may he be born in our hearts. Mary bore him in her womb; may we bear him in our hearts. The virgin became pregnant through the Spirit; may our souls be pregnant through faith in Christ. Our souls must bring forth God into the world."[2]

For Meister Eckhart we are all called to be virgins (fully open to the divine Spirit) and mothers (bringing forth God into this world). "I give birth to the one who gave birth to me." (Sermon, *Ave gratia plena*). This perspective of the Fathers and mystics of the Church helps us to perceive what is happening deep within us. Creation is experiencing the birth pangs of the divine Spirit, and this birthing takes place through human persons. Our consciousness is being transformed by the Spirit and elevated to a divine consciousness *just as* it came to a full blossoming in the consciousness of Jesus. We are being reborn in Christ, and we give birth to Christ in all the spheres of the christification process. It is in this process of christophany that we discover our true identity in answer to the question *who am I.*

What would be the concrete effect of theosis in human life? The person being reborn in God will be highly sensitive to the sufferings and agonies of people as well as of creation. We are all branches of one another on the one divine tree (I Jn. 1:7). One who lives from a divine centre of life will be a compassionate person. The face of God manifest in Jesus has been the compassionate face of God. By being inserted to the birthing of the Spirit one experiences the birth pangs of the new creation. In the lives of the poor and on the faces of the broken humans one discovers the healing presence of the God who creates everything anew. In their wounds, and in the woundedness of the mother earth, one discovers the *wounded*

---

[2] Quoted in Kurt Ruh, Meister Eckehart, C.H.Beck, Munich, 1985, 142.

God. At the same time one experiences the regenerative power of resurrection too in this broken world.

Advaita and Theosis

Let us return to the question put at the outset : *who am I?* The 'Spirit that searches the depth of God' (I Cor. 2:11) enables us to realise that we are being reborn in the Spirit and that we give birth to the Word in the world. Those who drink from the divine fountain unfolded in Jesus will be impregnated by the divine Spirit and hence will give birth to the new creation. (Jn.7:37-39). God gives birth to himself in and through us.

At the level of this mystical experience Christians meet the sages and seekers of the Indian heritage. The Upanishads and the later mystical traditions give witness to the experience of the sages who discovered their true identity within the inner-divine dynamics of *sat-chit-ananda* (Being-consciousness-bliss). They felt that they were being constantly transformed by the self-outpouring stream of divine life, and enlightened by the self-manifesting beam of divine light. They were led from the objectifying activity of the mind to the contemplative pursuits of the buddhi. Their consciousness was deepened and enlightened by the divine light. They could perceive the entire reality with its diversity in its ultimate depth of divine unity. *Prajnanam Brahma,* consciousness is divinised (Ait. Up. 3.3)- they could exclaim. Here the subject-object polarity is transcended. Here one discovers and realizes one's true nature as one with the divine nature. *"Brahmavid brahmaiva bhavati"* (the one who experiences the Divine *becomes* Divine. Mund. Up. 3.2.9) - this is the ultimate advaita-experience in the spiritual heritage of Indian sages. "Everyone united with the Lord *becomes* one Spirit with him" (I Cor. 6:17) - this is the deepest theosis-experience in the spiritual heritage of the Church. In the cave of the heart both seem to meet and merge into one!

5
CONTEMPLATION AND LIBERATIVE ACTION

A concrete way of getting our consciousness elevated to *theosis* is prayer. But the concept of prayer needs a certain refining to attune it to the mystical inward journey. Prayer is normally understood as consciously relating oneself to God either by words or in silence. Whether speaking to God or silently thinking of the Divine, the entire process of prayer normally evolves in a subject-object structure: for the praying person God becomes the *thou*, whom one addresses as *Father, Lord, Saviour, King or Master.* Such personalistic symbols have evolved out of the collective spiritual experience of a religious community like that of Israel or the Church or Islam. Hence these symbols are products of a culture that has its space-time configuration and consequent limitation. When the praying person tries to make any of these symbols one's own, a further moment of limitation comes in: the way one conceives God as Father or Saviour would depend very much on one's own existential situation. One tends to *project* the father or saviour, one is now in need of, onto the Divine and thereby to carve out an image of God that responds to one's needs here and now. Prayer would then mean bringing the Divine into the realm of inter-personal relationship and entering into dialogue with that God-for-me. Then it is no more a dialogue, but a monologue, since the dialogue-partner could be partly a projection of one's psyche. Hence the critics of religion called prayer an 'illusion' (Freud) a 'projection of the mind' (Feuerbach), a 'self-deception' (Marx), a 'disgrace to man' (Nietzsche) and 'something shameful to the human person' (Kant)! Here we touch upon a problem that not only calls in question the validity of prayer, but shakes the very foundation of theology.[1]

Is then prayer possible at all? One of the great masters of prayer said: "We do not know how we could pray properly!" (Rom. 8:26) This is a great insight. The Upanishadic master too spoke of this basic problem: "There the eye does not reach, nor speech nor mind" (Kena Up. 1.3). The first thought that should perhaps surface in our consciousness when we try to pray is that we are doing something humanly impossible. We can only sit and talk to a God whom we have managed to conceptualise as a *thou* for us; but finite words cannot really comprehend the infinite divine reality.

Paul does not leave the question there. He shows how genuine prayer evolves: "The divine Spirit comes to our help in our weakness and the Spirit prays in a way that cannot be expressed in words" (Rom. 8:26). The Upanishadic master too adds : 'that which cannot be attained by words, but that by which the word is expressed, seek That" (Kena Up. 1.5). Both these spiritual masters seem to suggest that we should go beyond the I-thou structure in the genuine process of prayer. God cannot just be brought down to the subject-object structure of our thought pattern in which prayer is supposedly to evolve as a dialogue between I and thou. The divine reality is beyond subject and object, and hence genuine prayer should be a spiritual process in which the I-thou structure is transcended. In such a process the praying person would realize that the God to whom one wants to pray is in fact the God who prays in-and-through the person. God is much more the subject than the object of prayer, nay he is beyond the subject-object polarity.

Left to ourselves we cannot transcend the subject-object structure of life and thought, nor can prayer be pressed into this scheme. The divine Spirit alone can reach the 'depths of God' (I Cor. 2:10; Rom. 11:33). Hence in prayer one has to be primarily silent in order to make room for the Spirit to pray, because it is in

---

[1] Painadath, Sebastian, SJ, *Dynamics of Prayer*, Asian Trading Corporation, Bangalore, 1980, 3

silence that the "groaning of the Spirit beyond words" can be heard (Rom. 8:23). Prayer then is basically a receptive process at the core of the human person. Only such an understanding of prayer can meet the problem of "psychic projection" and the other questions raised by the critics of religion. Prayer is a contemplative awareness of the transforming work of the Divine in all realms of human creativity. A revitalisation of the contemplative dynamics of prayer is an epochal need in meeting the challenge of the universal spiritual crisis and in overcoming the aberrations of certain popular devotions in religions.

Prayer as Articulation of Human Self-transcendence

Faced with the contemporary critique of prayer the question could be asked : Is prayer a constitutive factor of human life, or something just accidental and hence optional? This question cannot be discussed in relation to particular forms of prayer. One has to ask about the essential meaning of prayer in the integral growth of a human person.

An analysis of the structure of knowledge reveals the basic dynamics of the human mind. I can know a particular object only through participation and abstraction: my attention is focused totally on this particular object, but in the process of knowing, I abstract myself from this reality given before me. Through abstraction concepts are formed and through conceptualisation I as the knowing subject transcend the concrete object of knowledge. This is the spiritual capacity of a human being as knowing subject. No concrete object can really quench my existential quest for knowledge, which is ultimately open to the infinite dimensions of Truth. The fragmentary truth of any concrete object is known within the infinite horizon of the subject's structural openness to Truth-itself. Hence the explicit knowledge of particular objects presupposes an implicit awareness of the ultimate Truth that is immanent in encountering an object, but transcends it. The same could be said of our experience of beauty, love and goodness. The perception of something finite as finite is possible only with an implicit awareness of the Infinite, the Transcendent, the Beyond, the Being- itself.[2] This awareness may not easily surface in consciousness, but is at work latently in all the endeavours of human life causing a sort of creative restlessness. A master piece of artistic work, a musical melody, an elevating myth, a penetrating word or a peak experience in life may cause this depth-dimension to break into the surface of consciousness at least for a moment, with an enduring effect on a certain span of life.

The meaning of prayer can basically be found in this self-transcending dynamics of human life. Prayer is a conscious awakening to our constitutive orientation to the Beyond. In prayer one returns to the core of one's being and opens oneself to the transcendent horizon of one's life. In prayer one touches the Ground of being, the ultimate Ground of everything that exists. Through prayer one enters into the depth of reality and articulates the dimension of self-transcendence. Prayer is the awakening of the finite to the infinite, the state of being grasped by the transcendent power of Being-Itself.

Prayer as Awareness of the Divine Mystery

That unto which the human person is ultimately drawn, and that unto which we wake up in prayer, cannot be an it, an impersonal reality, nor can it be just a person, one among the many. That which gives ultimate meaning and fulfillment to human life can only be the supremely personal reality, the fullness of Being. The transcendent force behind the human quest for knowledge and love can only be the ultimate subject-and-object of knowledge-and-love. It can be called 'personal' only in an analogical sense; actually it is transpersonal. This reality of man's ultimate concern has been called in religious language 'the Divine', 'the Holy', God. This cannot be taken as a name given to the Nameless in view of objectifying it, but as a term that expresses the basis dynamics of the experience of the Ultimate. The Upanishadic term expresses it powerfully: *Brahman* means the *one* who is ever beyond (*brh* – to expand, grow, transcend).

---

[2] Rahner, Karl, SJ, Foundations of Christian Faith, London, 1978, 31-35

The Divine is an absolute mystery. The first and the last word we can have about the Divine is that we do not know him : *quod homo sciat se Deum nescire* (Thomas Aquinas, De pot. 7, 5, 14). No revelatory experience, no Holy Scripture, no religious tradition can raise any absolute claim of having fully comprehended the Divine mystery. "Our mental images hide God more than they reveal him" (Augustine). "God lives in inaccessible light, whom no one has seen, and no one is able to see" (I Tim. 6:16). The reality manifest in Jesus the Christ eludes the full human perception, for its "breadth and length, height and depth" is always beyond our grasp (Eph. 3:18).

The mystics of the Church constantly emphasised the apophatic character of our knowledge of the Divine. "If you know God, it is not God!" (Augustine, PL.8.663). In the entry of Moses into the darkness of the mountain Gregory of Nyssa finds the entry of the human into the "divine darkness". (Life of Moses, 376c-377a). Dionysius the Areopagite demands that the praying person has to "enter into the mysterious darkness of a holy ignorance." (Mystical Theology, 1,3). John Chrysostom invites Christians to "invoke the Divine as the inexpressible, incomprehensible, invisible and unknown reality." (Incomprehensibility of God, PG.3,166). For John Damascene too the Divine is primarily "infinite and incomprehensible." (PG. 94,800b) Evagrius of Pontus says about prayer : "When you pray let your intelligence take on the impression of no form; go immaterially to the Immaterial, and then you will understand what it is." (Chapters on Prayer, p.117). According to Meister Eckhart the praying person has to become 'godless' in order to experience God, for "God is beyond God."[3] In the book *The Cloud of Unknowing* there is a constant insistence on the need of putting the reason into the *cloud,* so that the divine Light from Beyond enlightens the intellect. For John of the Cross an experience of the "dark night of the soul" is an inevitable moment in the soul's ascent to God.

---

[3] Meister Eckhart, Deutsche Predigte und Traktate, Translated by Josef Quint, Diogenes, Muenchen, 1979, 304

This is a dimension that has been lost to a great extent in our speaking to God in prayer and in our speaking on God in theology. A religion that has lost its mystical depth has ceased to be a *religio*, for its structures, however well organised and effective they are, and its symbols, however magnificent and colourful they are, cannot any more be transparent media of communicating the experience of the Divine. India's spiritual heritage has constantly upheld this mystical dimension. The Upanishadic meditations on the Brahman evolve in a relentless pursuit of the Ineffable, the Incomprehensible, the Indescribable, the Unfathomable. (Brih. Up. 2.3.6, 4.2.4., 4.4.22.) The language of *bheda-abheda* is a powerful way of expressing the mystery character of the Divine: 'being and non-being', 'far and near', 'within and without', 'moving and unmoving', 'divided and undivided'. (Isa Up. 5,6; Mukti Up. 2,32, Gita, 9:19, 13:16)

Mystery does not mean distance. *Geheimnis*, the German word for mystery, means to be at home. The Divine as mystery is not a God far apart from us, a God up there. It is the divine presence felt most intimately in the inner core of our self that we experience as mystery. This can be seen in interpersonal relationships too: the more intimate someone becomes to us, the more does she/he come across to us as ineffable mystery. The actual core of the thou always eludes the grasp of the I, and thereby creates a constant fascination for the thou; there is always something *beyond* in the experience of genuine love. The closest person is the most mysterious one. The moment the mystery element vanishes, love becomes stale, and the other person gets reduced to a mere object that can be manipulated and exploited. This can happen in our relatedness to the Divine too: when the mystery dimension disappears prayer becomes stale and non-transformative; there is no more growth, for the divine reality has become more or less an idol in prayer. Actually the Divine is infinitely greater than our hearts and minds, our symbols and concepts, our religions and theologies, far beyond all that we made out of God. *Deus semper major*. Jesus taught his disciples to address the Divine as "Father in the heavens": an invocation that includes both an experience of deep intimacy

("Father") and a sense of awe before the unfathomable divine mystery ("in the heavens")

Prayer would then mean awareness of the Divine as incomprehensible mystery within and around us. It is a contemplative perception of one's being soaked in the divine presence; silence to the divine Silence. At this stage all concepts, images and symbols of God are left outside. One finds oneself "within the cave of the heart," "the inner castle of the soul," "in utter darkness or in dazzling light" - in both cases one is blinded by the ineffable mystery. (Mund.Up. 2.2.1, Swet. Up. 3.20, Kath Up. 4.6-7)

The Vedantic heritage of India is a challenge to Christians to enter into a deep contemplative experience of the divine mystery; only out of such a transcendental experience can we turn to the categorical symbols of faith.[4] Then there will be a creative dialectic between the awareness of the transpersonal Divine as mystery and the personal God as self-revealing. This would solve to a great extent the problem of psychic projection in prayer and stagnant anthropomorphism in theology. Meister Eckhart, the 'Christian Vedantin' of the 13th-14th century, once exclaimed: I let my God go for the sake of the Divine! [5]

Prayer as Awakening to the Inner-Trinitarian Process

Prayer, as we have seen, is an awareness of the ultimate depth of our being, the transpersonal mystery of the Divine. With this awareness there grows in the human person a quest for a revelatory experience: for a word from the divine silence, for a ray of light from the abysmal darkness, for an expression of love from the Beyond. Every religion in some way or other articulates this quest, and communicates an experience of the divine self-revelation as well. In every religion there is a dialectics between human quest and divine response expressed in its central symbols.

---

[4] Griffiths, Bede, Vedanta and Christian Faith, Dawn Horse, Clearlake, 1991, 85.

[5] Colledge/McGinn(ed), Meister Eckhart, Paulist,1981,New York, Introduction.

In the Christian faith-experience the divine mystery unfolds itself as Trinity: the Divine is Father, Son and Spirit as ONE. What is meant thereby is the dynamics of the self-communicating Life and Love of the Divine. This meaning can no longer be conveyed through an uncritical use of the traditional dogmatic formula of 'one substance and three persons'. Today we have a notion of person that is different from what the early Councils meant by terms like *hypostasis* or *persona* or *prosopon*.[6] For us today a person is an individual subject of independent consciousness having a distinct free will. When this notion is applied to the inner-divine dynamics of life we have no more the Trinity, but a tritheism: three *gods* before us. This can be noticed in popular Christian devotions and forms of prayer. One prays to the Father and to the Son (to Jesus) and to the Spirit, one being addressed after the other. The three persons of the Trinity thus become separate objects of devotion. This has led to a sort of compartmentalisation of the prayer life of many Christians.

The basic problem is that the persons of the Trinity have been too much individualised and objectified in the prayer process, and to a great extent made into objects of cult. The mystical aspect of participation in the divine life, as described by John, Paul and the early theologians of the Church, has been lost sight of. This can be solved only by going beyond the personalistic categories and transcending the subject-object structure of the theological thought pattern.

The ultimate source of faith in the Divine as Trinity is the inner experience of Jesus. In his contemplative intimacy with the divine Ground, Jesus experienced himself as the transparent medium transmitting divine life to the world. Hence he spoke of himself being the well which opens up the unseen springs within and pours out the water of divine life (Jn. 4:14; 7:37-38;5:26). He understood himself as the Word that gives articulation to the divine silence and communicates the meaning, the Truth (Jn. 5:37; 14:10; 15:26; 16:13). He described himself as the vinestock that grows out of the

---

[6] Rahner, Rahner, SJ, *Trinity*, in Sacramentum Mundi.

roots hidden in the mystery of the earth, and enables the vital sap to flow into the branches (Jn.15:1-5). He felt within him the flame that burns out of the hidden divine fire, and transmits heat and light to the world (Lk. 12:49; Jn. 3:19; 8:12; Rev. 2:18). The first Christian community experienced in Jesus the face of God turned towards humanity, the image of the unseen God, the embodiment of the concern of God, the outpouring of divine love into our hearts (Col. 1:15; Rom. 5:5, Jn. 3:16). God's love has been made manifest through the grace of the Son creating fellowship in the Spirit (I Cor. 12:12-14).

These symbols of the faith of the first Christian communities cannot just be pressed into personalistic categories as it happened in the history of theology and devotion across the centuries. They rather unfold the dynamics of the inner-trinitarian Life, moments of the self-outpouring of the divine Life-in-Love, modes of the existence of the Divine. The Father is the symbol of the ineffable, abysmal 'depth of God' (I Cor. 2:10); the Son stands for the moment of self-communication, unfolding of the depth; the Spirit is the power of divine Life-in-Love that emerges out of the divine depth of the Father and flows through the Son. One may speak of them as *subsisting relations* if this symbol does not evoke the idea of three objectified persons who could be addressed in prayer separately. The Father subsists only as 'the source' of the Son: the Son exists only as 'generated' by the Father; the Spirit is the 'power' that emerges out of this. What is important is to enter contemplatively into the inner experience of Jesus and perceive the dynamic unity of divine Life in its self-outpouring Love. This is possible only by revitalizing the contemplative dimension of prayer. [7]

Prayer would then mean a contemplative entry into the inner-trinitarian dynamics of Life-in-Love, a self-opening to the ongoing process of the divine self-outpouring. God as Trinity is not just God before us or above us, but within us; not so much a thou as I. God as Trinity means that the Divine continues to unfold itself creatively in and through us, There is a constant process of the

---

[7] Abhishiktananda, Saccidananda, ISPCK, Delhi, 1974, p.178.

'birth of God within our hearts': "the Father continuously gives birth to the Son and pours out the Spirit through us."[8] "Human existence springs from the very heart of the trinitarian mystery."[9] In contemplative prayer one touches not just the ground of one's own being, but the divine ground of everything that exists. It is an experience of koinonia from the dimension of depth: one finds oneself deeply bound with the lives of others like the branches of a tree, all emerging from the one divine source and root, supported by the one stem and enlivened by the one flow of vital sap, the Spirit (Jn. 15:1-4; I Cor. 12:4-11). Prayer makes a person experience oneself as the son/daughter through whom the Father constantly gives himself out in the Spirit. Prayer thus becomes a contemplative assimilation of the divine sonship manifest in Jesus the Christ, and an ecstatic perception of the fellowship brought about by the Spirit in the entire human family.

Prayer as Transparency to the Divine in Christ

Jesus lived and worked out of a deep intimacy with the divine Ground of being which he called the Father: The Father and I are ONE (Jn. 10:30). But this contemplative experience evolved in Jesus through a painful process: "During his life on earth Jesus offered up prayer and entreaty, aloud and in silent tears, to the one who had the power to save him out of death, and he submitted so humbly that his prayer was heard... Although he was Son, he learned obedience through suffering..." (Heb. 5:7). Jesus' total self-surrender to the Father meant total death to the ego in him, total life offered unto the divine Ground. He described this transformative process through an autobiographical symbol : "the grain of wheat has to fall on the ground and die, so that new life sprouts forth from it" (Jn. 12:24). His entire life was a continuous process of death and resurrection. Cross and Resurrection were not just events at the end of his life, but they meant the dialectical poles of an ongoing process of the human in him increasingly becoming transparent to the Divine in him.

---

[8] Meister Eckhart, in: Colledge, *op.cit.,* 54
[9] Abhishiktananda, *op.cit.,* 165

Jesus invited his disciples to follow him on the transformative
way of the Cross, which ultimately meant 'losing one's life' and
growing unto the Divine (Mk. 8:35). It was an invitation to enter
into the same transformative process that took place in him, so that
the disciples too experience oneness with the Father just as Jesus
experienced it:

Just as the Father knows me and I know the Father,
     I know my own and my own know me (Jn. 10:14-15);
Just as the Father loved me... and I remain in his love,
     I have loved you; remain in my love (Jn. 15:9-10; 17:23);
Just as the Father sent me into the world
     I have sent you into the world (Jn. 17:18);
Just as I draw life from my Father
     you too, will draw life from me (Jn. 6:57)
Just as I am in my Father and the Father is in me
     I am in you and you are in me (Jn. 14:20; 14:10; 6:56; 17:21);
Just as we are one
     may you be one in us, completely one (Jn. 17:21.23).

The Johannine expression *kathos* (just as) is of great theological
significance in understanding the relationship to Jesus the Christ:
the breakthrough of the Divine in Jesus is a process that should
happen in us too! Hence in our spiritual growth process, and in its
concrete articulation in prayer, Jesus the Christ is not just an object,
but much more the way, the truth and the life. In and through him
the way to the divine Ground has been opened through which the
mystery of the Divine has been unfolded to us (*alletheia*, truth,
in Greek, means unfolding), and the divine life made accessible.
Entry into this *way*, assimilation of this *truth* and participation in this
life is the Christological dimension of prayer. In fact all the Christ-
symbols of John are assimilative symbols, not meant for
objectification: bread is to eat and water to drink in order to assimilate
the inherent power; vinestock is not an object for the branches,
but their very subject and supporting medium of life-energy; light
is not what we see, but that in which we see everything; the shepherd
in John chapter 10 is not someone who stands apart but lets his
life merge with that of the sheep. With these symbols the
mystic evangelist presents Jesus not as someone before us in

the process of prayer, but as the divine power within us. Prayer consists in being transparent to the breakthrough of this power.

Paul too presents Jesus the Christ as the outpouring of the divine power: the Lord is the Spirit (II Cor. 3:17). His entire Christology could be summarised in the key phrase *in Christo*. For Paul life emerges, evolves and finds fulfillment in Christ (Rom. 6:3-11,23; 8:2,39; I Cor. 1:4; II Cor. 5:17; Gal. 2:4,20; 3:28; Phil. 4:21; Col. 1:27; 2 Tim. 2:1). A contemplative awakening to the evolution of life in Christ led Paul to the ecstatic exclamation: "For me life is Christ....I live, not I, Christ lives in me!" (Phil. 1:21; Gal. 2:20).

Hence the Christological dimension of prayer consists not merely in praying to Jesus, but much more in praying *in Christ*.[10] Prayer is a contemplative participation in the transformative process that took place in Jesus the Christ. In prayer one experiences oneself as the channel of the Spirit of the new creation, as the well or stream that communicates divine life to the world (Jn. 7:38), as the branch of the tree that grows out of the divine root and bears fruits manifest in Jesus (Jn. 15:5), as the instrument for continuing the divine work of recreation initiated in Jesus the Christ (Jn. 14:12). Prayer is the total personal surrender in the divine Ground as it happened in Jesus, a death to the possessive ego-sense and resurrection to the inner divine dynamics of Spirit-generated rebirth (Jn. 3:5; Rom. 6:5 Phil. 3:10). Through prayer a person becomes increasingly transparent to the Divine presence so that the Divine can fully take possession of the person. Prayer is thus the awakening of the human to the inner transformative process of "getting filled with the utter fullness of God" as manifest in Jesus the Christ (Eph. 3:19).

Prayer as Letting the Spirit Pray

The power of this transformative process is the divine Spirit poured out in Jesus the Christ. Jesus lived out of the experience that the

---

[10] cfr. E Malatesta SJ, Jesus Christ in the History of Devotion, Religious Series, Vol. 1

Spirit guided him to carry out the work of the Father (Lk. 4:14,18; 10:21; Mt.12:28); he promised his disciples that the same Spirit would be "with them for ever" to "liberate them," to "lead them to the fullness of Truth" and to "enable them to carry out the same works" (Jn. 8:32;14:17;16:13;14:12). Prayer would then mean a contemplative awareness of this transformative presence of the divine Spirit within oneself and all around. Prayer is sensitivity to the Spirit. At the core of his being the praying person listens to the ecstatic cry of the Spirit, Abba! (Gal. 4:6, Rom. 8:15). This self-awakening takes place not in so many words, but in deep silence. Hence Paul says that the prayer of the Spirit cannot be put into words; it emerges from a transpersonal source and hence expresses itself in a metalogical form : through groanings. Prayer would then consist in becoming aware of the groaning of the Spirit from within our hearts, in listening to "the Spirit praying in a way that cannot be expressed in words" (Rom. 8:26-27). To pray means to let the Spirit pray. The God to whom we want to pray is in fact the God who prays in and through us.[11] The subject-object structure of our thought pattern is transcended by the Spirit: by the Spirit alone, for it "reaches the depths of the Divine" (I Cor. 2:10). The Holy Spirit is the ultimate *subject* of genuine prayer.[12]

But the Spirit reaches not only the depth of the Divine but also the farthest horizons of creation. Paul develops a cosmic theology of prayer: the entire creation is continuously groaning for the experience of ultimate liberation; we too are groaning within creation for the freedom of the children of God, and the Spirit also groans within us! (Rom. 8:18-27). Paul purposely uses the term 'groaning' to emphasise both the acuteness of suffering and the power of hope; it is like the cry of a woman in birth-pangs. In the entire realm of creation Paul perceives the painful process of the birth of a new creation. The divine Spirit is to be experienced within this process, as suffering within creation and at the same time transforming it into a new being. The presence of the Spirit in the

---

[11] cfr. Painadath, Sebastian SJ, Dynamics of Prayer, ATC, Bangalore, 1980, 209-220

[12] cfr. Abhishiktananda, Prayer, ISPCK, Delhi, 1972.

world therefore means that God participates in the sufferings of humanity and overcomes suffering through the power of divine love. Prayer as the contemplative perception of the groaning of the Spirit would then mean opening oneself to the God who suffers in the world as revealed in the crucified Christ, and transforms this world into the new being manifest in the risen Christ.

Prayer as Participation in the Liberative Process

Practically all forms of prayer evolve with a preconceived picture of God. Religions universally speak of God as the Almighty to whom we could cry out in our afflictions, for he is beyond suffering and history. With this picture of God however we cannot grasp the specific aspect of the Divine manifest in the crucified Christ: "The crucifixion of Christ cannot be expressed in philosophical terms at all!" (I Cor. 1:17). The Cross puts all our philosophical notions of God upside down. The Divine manifest in the crucified Christ is not the God up there on the peak of bliss, but the One who moves with us in the valley of tears, a God not beyond history, but within the historical process, a God not on the other shore, but struggling with us in the whirlpools of suffering. Emmanuel, God-with-us, that is his 'name' (Mt. 1:23).

On the cross God revealed himself as the suffering God : the "weakness of God" and the "foolishness of God" have been made manifest. Such a God challenges the speculative patterns of philosophers and disappoints the devotional fantasies of pious people (I Cor. 1:22-25). On the cross was revealed the wound hidden in the Divine, the wound created by human sinfulness. The *first sin* meant not only a wound in the human race (symbol 'original sin'), and in the cosmos (felt through all sorts of estrangements), but much more a woundedness in God. The history of salvation is the history of God pursuing humanity with a wounded heart. Jesus portrayed this powerfully in the picture of the wounded father (Lk. 15:11-32) and in his other parables of God's pathos (Lk. 13:34-5; 14:15-24; 15:4-10; 20:9-19). If God is Love he has to be a vulnerable God, a suffering God: an invulnerable person cannot genuinely love. This understanding of theopathy is important for the right perception of prayer. Out of the depths of afflictions we cannot just call to a God out there, we can only take refuge in a God who is with us in the midst of suffering. He is not the Lord above our heads, but the *slave* who washes our feet! (Jn. 13:1-15; Mk. 10:42). This is the revolutionary, and perhaps the specific, picture of God in Christian faith. It is the God who identifies himself with the suffering humanity: "I was hungry,......I was thirsty,...I was homeless....I was sick..." (Mt. 25:35-36). As long as there is poverty, suffering, sickness and oppression, all caused ultimately by human sin, we can only speak of a God who suffers with us, in us and because of us. This is the paradox of the Christian experience of the Divine : no spirituality, no prayer, if it is to be authentically Christian, can bypass this paradox.[13]

But the life of Jesus did not end with the cross, he rose up overcoming the powers of evil. The Resurrection unfolds the transforming power of divine love. It gives us the experience of a God who is with us removing the forces of alienation and suffering; it gives us the assurance that ultimately "God will be all in all" (I Cor. 15:28), that everything will be led to its final restoration in the Christ (Col. 1:15-20: Eph. 1:10; 3:19). The Resurrection of Jesus is a pointer to the ultimate cosmic resurrection, the process which evolves through the creative interaction between God and man in history. God's Spirit manifest in the risen Lord is at work in the world creating "a new heaven and a new earth", and we are called to participate in this work of regeneration (II Cor. 5:17; Rev. 21:1). The reality that evolves through this God-man dialectics is what Jesus called the Kingdom of God: the state of being in which the entire creation becomes transparent to the Divine presence, the entire world becomes one theophany; it is the situation of justice and peace, freedom and fellowship.

Prayer would then mean awareness of the divine Spirit participating in the sufferings of the world and transforming this world into the reality of the Kingdom of God. A contemplative

---

[13] cfr. Moltmann, Juergen, The Crucified God, SCM, London, 1987, 329-332.

entry into the divine Ground of being makes a person discover the wound hidden in God, and with that perception one sees the same wound opening up in the wounded people around and in the wounded earth as well. At the same time contemplation makes one perceive the transforming power of the divine love and experience its creative movements in the liberative endeavours of people. Prayer thus becomes an awakening of the person to the suffering and transforming presence of the Divine manifest in the cross and Resurrection of Jesus the Christ and continuing to manifest itself in the sufferings of the people as well as in their creative initiatives to overcome suffering. Contemplative prayer is not inertia to human suffering, but it makes a person increasingly sensitive to the suffering of others because one perceives it from the depth of reality, and not as something alien to oneself or to God. Thus prayer becomes a cry of human suffering and a quest for liberation. This is powerfully expressed in Jesus' prayer in agony: My God, My God, why have you forsaken me! At the same time prayer makes a person courageous to challenge the structures of oppression, imaginative to commit oneself to the integral liberation of people out of a deep conviction that God is at work in this liberative process. To pray means to attune oneself to the will of God who transforms our life. The mystical awareness of the Divine engenders prophetic dynamism; the return to the divine centre evokes tremendous centrifugal forces in life. Prayer helps a person develop a divine perspective on life and world: to pray is to see everything as God sees it; to pray means to see God in all things and all things in God. (Ignatius Loyola, Spir. Exer. §235)

With this perception, prayer can be understood as participation in the liberative dynamics of the Divine in the world. This is the meaning of action out of contemplation. It is action charged with a heightened sense of responsibility, for the person finds himself or herself co-responsible with God for the integration of the world. Action out of contemplation is not motivated by vested interests or psychic needs, but exclusively by the demands of the ever widening horizons of the Kingdom of God. Through contemplative prayer a transference of the centre of the person takes place : from ego-centredness to God-centredness, from *ahamkara* to *atmabodha*. Only in the measure in which such a liberation, and consequent integration, takes place in the person can he or she be engaged in a truly liberative action. Otherwise the question will always remain: who will liberate the liberator?

The fruits of contemplation are courage, creativity and compassion. When through integral contemplation the centre of action is shifted from *ego* to the true *self,* one is attuned to the divine Spirit, that makes the person courageous to face the challenges of life. "Fearlessness is the fruit of spirituality", Mahatma Gandhi said. Once freed from fear one becomes creative in responding to the demands of the life process within the Divine. One is enabled to explore the ever new ways of responding to the inspirations of the Spirit in creating a better world. Contemplative introspection unfolds creative potentialities. In this process however compassion will be the hallmark of a contemplative person. Through compassion one makes oneself a channel of divine love. Through our compassionate dealings God's compassion touches the hearts of people and instils hope. Contemplation becomes liberative through the courage of creativity and gentleness of compassion.

6

CHURCH AS THE CONTINUATION OF THE MEAL-FELLOWSHIP OF JESUS

Reflection on the mystery of the Church has been a central theme of theology in recent years. This has special significance in the multi-religious and pluri-cultural continent of Asia. The II.Vatican Council in its foundational document *Lumen Gentium* mentions several images of the Church, viz. God's sheepfold and field, vineyard and house, temple and city; Christ's mystical body and bride; our mother and teacher, the budding forth of the Kingdom of God and the sacrament of the unity of humanity, the new Israel and the pilgrim people of God. (LG. 5.6.8.9. cfr. SC.26) All these symbols point to the spiritual substance of the Church. Each of these brings out a particular dimension of what the Church has to become. When we examine the original praxis of Jesus his vision about the Church as the community of his disciples becomes clearer. An integral element of his praxis has been his *meal-fellowhip with the publicans and sinners.* We meet him often breaking bread with the outcasts of society, thereby sharing with them his vision about the new society: blessed are the poor, for they will inherit the Kingdom of God. The meal-fellowship of Jesus with the publicans and sinners shows clearly how the Jesus community emerged concretely from the living realities of the people, from among the poor and the low-caste sectors. Hence a reflection on this element of the praxis of Jesus would bring us to the real *birthplace* of the Church. Could we then understand the Church, that Jesus dreamed, as the continuation of what evolved in and through his meal-fellowship with the poor?

A powerful global consciousness is growing today. The whole world is shrinking into a global village, in which everyone seems to know everyone else. Nations are coming closer together and people are intermingling beyond borders; cultures intersect one another and religions interact on a wider spectrum. Communication technologies and travel facilities bring peoples into a global networking much more than ever before. What affects any one part of the earth or a particular nation has decisive consequences for the entire humanity. In the growth of this global consciousness the ethical values of freedom and fellowship, equality and solidarity emerge with a new intensity and universal significance. On this global scene religions cannot any more be divisive powers, but really unifying forces. It is in this process that the Church has to rediscover her meaning and mission. Here too the egalitarian values and spiritual attitudes which evolved from the meal-fellowship of Jesus are of great significance. In terms of the meal-fellowship of Jesus the Church could understand her mission as a transforming presence in the world that seeks a spiritual potential in the emerging global consciousness. Church could function as a *leaven* in socio-cultural life, as a *sign* of prophetic critique as well as *light* for mystical introspection. In India where the divisive and unitive forces of religions are battling against each other the meal-fellowship of Jesus inspires us to act as a reconciliatory presence.

In order to grasp the liberative potential of the meal-fellowship of Jesus we need to examine its socio-cultural context:

The Social Background of Jesus

Jesus lived in a predominantly Jewish society. A basic principle of the Jewish existence was its vocation-consciousness: 'we are the people chosen by God, not the others' (Exod. 19:5; Deut. 7:7-11; 26:19). Jews took pride in their status of being a 'kingdom of priests, a consecrated nation' (Exod. 19:6). It was for them a call and a responsibility: they felt called 'to be holy, for Yahweh is holy' (Lev. 11:45). Out of this passion for holiness gradually emerged a compulsive concern to observe the complex rules regarding the clean and the unclean. (Lev. 11-16). In course of time the Jewish religion developed an elaborate system of purificatory rites and rituals centred around the Temple. The Prophets of Israel however upheld the concern of justice and love above ritualistic practices. (Is.1:15-18; 58:6; Mic. 6:6-8; Amos 5:21-25). The exile in Babylon came to be understood as a punishment of the Lord for disloyalty to the Covenant. After returning from the exile one of the major concerns of the Jewish people was to regain the lost racial purity and re-establish the religious integrity of the community. Through a social scanning those who had not polluted their blood 'by marrying a foreign man or woman' were identified and gradually a religious elite evolved through them. They claimed to be the *pure* sector of Israel within the Jewish community. (Cfr. Ezra 9:9-10; Neh. 9:2)

At the time of Jesus the consciousness of racial purity was very strong among the elite. Those who could prove that at least since five generations nobody from their ancestral line had married any non-Jew could claim to belong to the stratum of the *pure.* Only from their circles could any one become a teacher, priest, judge or leader of the community. The majority that could not establish the racial purity was considered the *impure,* however within the milieu of the people of God.[1]

Besides the purity of blood there were also other factors which determined one's social status in life. "There was a whole series of trades which were despised, and those who practised them were, to a greater or lesser degree, exposed to social degradation."[2] To such unholy trades belonged ass-drivers, camel-drivers, sailors, shopkeepers and herdsmen; these were called the 'crafts of robbers' because those who took to them were prone to dishonesty and swindle. Dung-collectors, metal-smelters, launderers, weavers, tanners and butchers worked in places with a foul smell and hence these were also impure jobs. Professions associated with the human body carried the stigma of immoral practices and financial exploitation; hence barbers, physicians, nurses and bath attendants were considered impure. There were many prostitutes, who were mostly

---

[1] Jeremias, Joachim, *Jerusalem in the Time of Jesus,* SCM, London, 1985, 275- 302.

[2] *Ibid.,* 303.

women divorced for silly reasons or by force. Peddlers and gamblers made themselves impure by trading with coins having a pagan icon; tax collectors were hated for they exploited the native Jews and supported the hegemony of the pagan Roman power in the Jewish land. No good Jew at the time of Jesus would engage in any of these despised trades and those involved in them were all called the *impure*. Maladies like leprosy and haemorrhage were considered polluting; epilepsy and insanity were attributed to the work of evil spirits. Lepers and those possessed by evil spirits were ousted from the community and forced to live on funeral spots, in isolated valleys or in the wilderness. Even the deaf and the lame, the blind and the crippled were sometimes considered *impure* for they carried the punishment of their sins or the stigma of the sins of their parents. (Cfr. John 9:2, Lk. 14:21) All these sections of Jews marginalised through impurity of blood, unholy trades and cursed infirmities formed the *impure* stratum at the bottom of the social system.[3]

In order to denote the sector of the *pure* Jews the Gospels use the term *scribes and pharisees;* the *impure* people are designated *publicans and sinners.* The term *sinners* meant not just those who committed sins, but those who took to trades which were prone to sinful practices or those who through certain infirmities carried the effects of sin in their body and mind.[4] What characterised the social fabric of the country of Jesus was a sort of *caste system* : the scribes and pharisees, the people of the upper caste, looked down upon the publicans and sinners, those belonging to the lower caste. Since the administrative machinery with the legal competence was reserved to the members of the upper stratum the elite could wield authority over the masses, who were pejoratively called 'the rabble that does not know the law' (*amha-aretz*). The upper caste Jews felt that they were closer to God, because they knew the intricacies of the Law and observed them meticulously; they claimed that they formed the *pure* community of the Covenant, the true Israel. They would not easily associate themselves with the low

---

[3]   *Ibid.,* 311

[4]   Fitzmeyer, Joseph A, SJ, The Gospel according to Luke, Vol II, Anchor Bible, Doubleday, New York, 1985, 1075.

caste people of the community due to prejudices based on purity laws.

A pharisee or scribe would not like to visit the home of a tax collector (Lk.19:7) or stay with him at prayer (Lk. 18:13) for the latter was looked down upon as a sinner. He would refuse to let a sinful woman enter his house (Lk. 7:39); for him a leper is an untouchable person (Mk.1:41) and a man possessed with evil spirit is someone to be totally shunned (Mk.5:3) A Jew of the upper stratum would not willingly buy provisions from the shop of someone of lower social order; if at all he buys something, he would throw out one-tenth of every packet in order to make sure that the rest is made pure by paying the tithe (Lk. 11:42). On returning from the market place presumably polluted by the footprints of the *impure* people the scribes and pharisees would 'never eat without first sprinkling themselves' (Mk. 7:4). And before every meal they observed the strict ritual practices of 'washing their arms as far as the elbow' and 'cleaning the outside of cup and dish' (Lk. 11:39). Such socio-religious customs point to an elitist culture that prevailed with a social bias among the scribes and pharisees.

This cream-layer mentality was most evident in the way the scribes and pharisees took their meals. In religious persuasion meal-fellowship was 'the high point of their life as a group.'[5] To have meal-fellowship with someone meant to break bread with the other, to share one's life with the other, to look at the other as of equal dignity and respect, the other as brother or sister. It was an expression of intimacy and equality, fellowship and solidarity. Besides, the meal-fellowship on the earth was considered to be a sacred function, a 'fellowship before God', for it symbolised the messianic banquet with the great forefathers at the table of the Lord. (Is. 25:6; 55:1-3; Ps. 23:5; cfr. Mt. 8:11, Lk. 22.30) One would imagine that only the chosen ones of the Lord would be invited to this heavenly meal, and consequently only those who were considered to be *pure* were invited on earth to the meal-fellowship of the social and religious

---

[5] Neusner, Jacob, Formative Judaism: Religious, Historical and Literary Studies, Scholars Press, Chicago, 1985, 76.

aristocracy. Therefore the upper caste Jews would not like to invite those of the lower strata to their meals and family celebrations. This apathy is expressed in the protest of Simon the pharisee on the entry of the sinful woman to his dining hall (Lk. 7: 39). This is also seen in the reaction of the Pharisees to Jesus' option to visit Zachaeus the tax-collector (Lk.19:7). Jesus portrays this pharisaic mentality in the refusal of the *elder son* to have meal-fellowship with his younger brother, who returned from an irregular way of life. (Lk. 15:28)

Jesus's Reaction

Jesus entered this broken society with a deep sense of divine mission: "The Spirit of the Lord has anointed me and sent me to bring good news to the poor, to proclaim liberty to the captives and to the blind new sight, to set the downtrodden free, to proclaim the Lord's year of favour" (Lk.4:18-19). He acted out of the abiding consciousness that he was doing the Father's work: "The works which I do are not my works; the Father in me does his works." (Jn.5:36; 10:25; 8:28). With this sense of divine mission Jesus confronted the local religiosity with clarity and courage. Whenever someone in need approached Jesus he would forget most of the prohibitions related to traditions and customs. Ignoring all forms of social bias he would meet every person in his / her concrete existential situation. He would relativise everything in favour of a human person: law and religion, sabbath and temple, purity rites and social customs, even the ritual forms of worshipping God. (Mk. 3:4; Jn. 4:23).

In unambiguous terms Jesus upheld the integral human concern above all religious practices: "Sabbath is for the human person, not the human person for sabbath" (Mk. 2:27). "Love is far more important that any holocaust" (Mk. 12:33). "What God demands is mercy, not sacrifice" (Mt. 12:7). Reconciliation with the brothers and sisters should go prior to all offerings (Mt. 5,23). Compassion for the wounded human being is more salutary than passion for ritual purity (Lk. 10:36). Compassion for the suffering person is more important than purity measures and legal observances (Jn. 8:7). Concern for human liberation is far more important than legal observances (Lk. 13:12). Justice is of a higher value than the paying of tithes (Lk. 11:42). Love should overcome every caste bias (Lk. 19:5). Man is of greater worth than Sabbath. (Jn. 9:14).

In his dealings with people Jesus was very unconventional, quite unorthodox. Jesus sought out Zachaeus, the *sinner* and went to his home (Lk. 19:5) . Jesus stretched out his hand and touched the *untouchable* leper (Lk. 5:13). He welcomed the entry of the *impure* woman into the dining hall of the pharisee (Lk. 7:44).He liberated the *sinful* woman from the oppressive grips of the law (Jn. 8:11). These and many other instances show how affectionately Jesus dealt with the human persons of the *impure* strata and freed them from the tragic consequences of a discriminative social system. In a sense Jesus radicalised the old Levitical precept, *be holy because Yahweh is holy* (Lev. 19:2) with his principle, *be merciful as the heavenly Father is merciful.* (Lk. 6:36) [6]

Compassion is the Heart-beat of Holiness

This stance of Jesus is most evident in his meal-fellowship with the publicans and sinners. As he found that the brokenness of the Jewish community caused by a betrayal of the messianic values was concretely felt at the breaking of the bread, Jesus started a liberative *movement:* his meal-fellowship. To his meals Jesus would welcome people of all social strata especially the poor and the marginalised ones. He would affectionately recline with them on the floor, compassionately break with them the one bread and courageously proclaim to them the values of the new community that he envisaged: the community of the Kingdom of God. This has not been a rare practice on special occasions in the pubic life of Jesus, but a habitual way of mixing with the common people. "If his mission was directed exclusively to sinners (Mk. 2:17) he must have habitually sought their company and

---

[6] Soares-Prabhu, George SJ, The Table Fellowship of Jesus, Its Significance for Dalit Christians in India Today, *in* Isaac Padinjarekuttu(ed) The Collected Writings of Goerge Soares Prabhu SJ, Vol 1, Biblical Themes for a Contextual Theology Today, Jnana-Deepa Vidyapeeth, Pune, 1999, 229.

expressed his solidarity with them in the customary manner, namely, by eating and drinking with them."[7] "It is quite certain that Jesus did habitually dine with the religious and social outcasts of his society, even though this behaviour of his aroused sharp and sustained criticism from the religious elite. References to such table-fellowship are found in all the commonly recognised strands of the Synoptic tradition, in Mk. 2:16-17, in *Q* (Mt. 11:16-19; Lk. 7:31-35) and in the special material of Luke (15:1ff) and Mathew (21:31ff). Such wide references to a subject which must have been a cause of considerable embarrassment to his first followers suggest that Jesus' table-fellowship with the outcasts was not only a well-known, historically certain feature of his ministry, but a highly significant feature as well."[8] Because of Jesus' habitual sharing of meal with the publicans and sinners he was given a nickname by the scribes and pharisees: 'a glutton and drunkard, a friend of tax collectors and sinners'.(Mt. 11:19) "The table fellowship is one of the most conspicuous and controversial aspects of the renewal movement founded by Jesus."[9]

The meal-fellowship of Jesus has been the *Sitz im Leben* of many prophetic utterances of Jesus, for his intimacy with the poor was most manifest in his shared meals with them. Even if the direct association of these sayings with the meal context cannot be established, they do get a deeper meaning when they are read in the context of this original praxis of Jesus. To the publicans and sinners dining with him Jesus would say: "Blessed are you poor: yours is the Kingdom of God. Blessed are you, who are hungry now: you shall have your fill" (Lk. 6:20). The radical meaning of this proclamation resonates in what he said: "Tax collectors and prostitutes are making their way into the Kingdom of God before (those who claim to be the just and the pure)" (Mt. 21:31). "Many

---

[7] Kappen, Sebastian SJ, Table-Fellowship as Socialist Praxis, in: Jesus and Society, (Selected Writings of S.Kappen, edited by S.Painadath SJ), ISPCK, 2002, 85.

[8] Soares, *op.cit.*, 225

[9] Borg, Marcus, J, Conflict, Holiness and Politics in the Teaching of Jesus, Mellen, New York, 1984, 80

will come from east and west and sit down with Abraham and Isaac and Jacob at the feast of the Kingdom of God; but the children of the Kingdom will be thrown out into the darkness outside," (Mt. 8:11). With these words Jesus has been announcing the breaking in of a new age, the messianic era, in which the poor and the marginalised will have priority over the socially elite and the religiously pure sections. "Many who are first will be last, and last will be first." (Mt. 19:30; 20:16; Lk.13:30; Mk.10:31). The meal-fellowship of Jesus is a prophetic critique on the *pyramidal* society, in which one sits over the head of the other in order to 'lord authority over the others' (Mk10:42). Instead, Jesus envisaged a *circular* society, in which all irrespective of social bias and religious purity would sit shoulder to shoulder, break the *one* bread and share the *one* meal, thus embodying solidarity with all in the *one* humanity. This new social order will be characterised by the readiness to be a 'slave to all' (Mk.10:44) the humility to 'wash one another's feet' (Jn. 13:14), the willingness to 'take the lowest seat' (Lk. 14:10).

Parables in the Context of the Meal-fellowship

The parable of the *prodigal* son (which is actually the parable of the *dutiful* son) has been told during a meal with the impure ones. (Lk. 15:1) As Jesus was affectionately sharing meal with the publicans and sinners, there came a strong protest from the pharisees and scribes: this man welcomes sinners and even eats with them! (Lk. 15:2). It is in response to them that Jesus told this parable. Though three parables are found in this chapter Luke speaks of only one parable (note the *singular* in 15:3). Hence the parables of the lost sheep and that of the lost drachma must have been later additions to this chapter.[10] Luke's introduction pointing to the shared meal has to be taken as immediately referring to the parable given in vv. 11-32. Hence the meal-fellowship with publicans and sinners could be taken as the *Sitz im Leben* of this parable. It is the

---

[10] Fitzmeyer, Joseph A, SJ, The Gospel according to Luke, Vol II, Anchor Bible, Doubleday, New York, 1985, 1076.

dutiful elder son that represents the hearers, namely the pharisees and scribes. (Lk.15:3) As the younger brother returned home after an unholy life he was an *impure* person. The elder one, who claimed never to have forfeited his loyalty and *purity,* could not consider the other one as his own brother: note the expression, 'this son of yours' (Lk.15:30). He refused to go in to eat with him (Lk.15:28). His language of justifying himself on the basis of adherence to the law, of condemning the other for reasons of loose life and of demanding reward from the father for his meticulous obedience betrays the language of the pharisees and scribes (Lk. 15:29-30). Through the portrait of the dutiful elder son Jesus unmasks the hardheartedness and cynicism of his critics as he was having meal-fellowship with the impure ones of society. The complaint of the indignant pharisees and scribes ('this fellow welcomes sinners' Lk. 15:2) is reflected in the protest of the elder son ('this son of yours returning from a loose life' Lk.15:3). Their reluctance to break bread with the outcasts is similar to his refusal to dine with the younger brother. In both cases we do find prejudicial attitudes and judgemental statements with a pejorative tone. The divine mercy symbolised in the compassionate father embraces the estranged without making calculations and takes home the repentant one without putting conditions. The publicans and sinners invited to share meal with Jesus must have constantly felt this divine mercy embodied in Jesus. The meal-fellowship of Jesus presented a God who demands compassion, not adherence to rituals and laws (cfr. Mt. 12:7; Lk. 10:31-33)

Luke narrates another parable which was also told during a meal (Lk. 14:15-24). As the invited guests did not turn up, the master of the house asks the servants: go out into the streets and alleys of the town and bring in the poor, the crippled, the blind and the lame (Lk. 14:21). This scene describes the way how God welcomes the poor to communion with him. Those who were first invited belonged to the chosen race, but their minds got so much stuck in commercial matters that they could not any more respond to God's invitation (Lk. 14:18). They betrayed the Covenant and lost the fellowship with God. Hence the time has come that the doors of the messianic community are now open wide to the poor and the gentiles. The verdict has fallen: 'not one of those who were originally invited shall have a taste of my banquet' (Lk. 14:24). This critique of God and the consequent new order of realities are manifest in the meal-fellowship of Jesus with publicans and sinners. The ethics of this new order is presented by Jesus in unambiguous terms: "When you give a meal, do not invite your friends or your brothers or your relations or rich neighbours, in case they invite you back and so repay you. No, when you give a meal, invite the poor, the crippled, the lame, the blind; then you will be blessed, for they have no means to repay you and so you will be repaid when the upright rise again." (Lk. 14:12-14). The meal-fellowship of Jesus presents a God who forgives and justifies the sinners, and communes with the *impure*. What enables access to God's life is not racial purity or observance of laws but unconditional trust in God's providence; and the poor are more sensitive to this.

Towards a Counter-culture

By breaking bread with the poor and the marginalised Jesus made clear that God's ways are different from man's calculations. "The inclusion of sinners in the community of salvation, achieved in table fellowship, is the most meaningful expression of the message of the redeeming love of God."[11] God's mercy surpasses man's logic. No one needs to go to God with the claim of good works and demand remuneration (Lk. 18:11). "Not anyone who says *Lord, Lord*, will enter the Kingdom of God, but the one who does the will of God" (Mt. 7:21). No one can stand before God with the claim of 'having worked many miracles in God's name' (Mt.7:22). No one will be justified before God on the basis of a meticulous observation of the law (Lk. 18:14). The human cannot fix standards for the working of the divine grace (Mt.20:15). We cannot determine the route along which the divine Spirit blows (Jn.3:8). God does not act to the tune of human music (Lk.7:32). At the meal-fellowship with Jesus the poor experienced concretely the infinite

---

[11] Jeremias, Joachim, New Testament Theology, Vol. I. SCM. London, 1971,116.

goodness of the heavenly Father who loves all, the good and evil doers, the upright and the wicked, the *pure* and the *impure* (Mt. 5:45). They felt accepted by the merciful God. In Jesus they recognised the compassionate face of God turned towards them: the 'son of man who came to seek and save what was lost' (Lk. 19:10). "It is this encompassing compassion of God that the table-fellowship of Jesus reveals."[12] With the meal-fellowship Jesus was thus presenting a new culture, a *counter-culture*, the culture of the Kingdom of God. He was initiating a movement of spirituality, not establishing a structure of religion. He was helping people to respond to the movement of the divine Spirit in the given situation, not asking them just to adhere to the purity laws and ritual traditions of a particular religion. Through the meal-fellowship Jesus created *space* for the Spirit of God to work in the hearts of persons and to transform the structures of society. If the Spirit of the Son sets you free, you are free indeed! - this is the abiding message of the meal-fellowship of Jesus (cfr. Jn. 8:36).

An increasing number of common people experienced the liberative power and presence of the divine Spirit in their lives. In the experience of being respected by Jesus they felt a new sense of worth: they could accept themselves as accepted by God. They came to know that they were not condemned to live as *slaves* on the fringe of society but called to assert themselves as *children* of God (Jn. 8:11). They were liberated from a sense of being unwanted to a sense of self-worth based on the experience of being embraced by God. They realised that, even if they were marginalised by the established religion, they had a right to take pride in being the spiritual heirs of the Kingdom of God. A new vocation consciousness emerged in them: we are the inheritors of the Kingdom of God, we are the 'heirs of God' (Lk. 22:28-30; Rom. 8:17).

This new awakening in the people meant a threat to those in authority. In the beginning the aristocracy just ignored the movement that grew around the meal-fellowship of Jesus for

---

[12] Soares, *op.cit.*, 233.

they thought 'nothing good could come from Nazareth' (Jn.1:46). The scribes and pharisees knew well that 'prophets would not arise in Galilee' (Jn. 7: 52). Later they started complaining to the disciples: 'why does your master eat with tax collectors and sinners?'(Mt.9:11; Lk.15:2). Gradually they found that the meal-fellowship of Jesus was becoming a rallying point where the downtrodden were regaining a new sense of worth. So they started calumniating Jesus: 'he is a glutton and a drunkard, a friend of tax collectors and sinners' (Lk. 7:35). They found him 'possessed by Beelzebub, the prince of devils' (Lk.11:15; Jn.8:48, 52). They questioned his divine authority (Mk.11:28) and tried to arrest him (Jn. 7:44; 11:57). Some even picked up stones to throw at him (Jn.8:59; 10:31). In spite of all this the number of people who felt attracted to the meal-fellowship of Jesus only increased. Those in authority were then compelled to ask themselves: "What action are we taking? If we let him go on in this way everybody will believe in him , and the Romans will come and suppress the Holy Place and our nation!" (Jn. 11:47-48). The Sanhedrin was getting quite panicky about the impact of the meal-fellowship of Jesus on the people. The religious aristocracy feared that it would lose its hold on the masses. Those in authority found that the emergence of a spiritual consciousness among the people would mean the crumbling of the power structures of the Jewish religion. Hence came the nervous reaction of Caiaphas, the high priest: "You do not seem to have grasped the seriousness of the situation at all. It is better that one man dies for the people than the whole nation going to pieces." (Jn. 11:50) . So they took the decision to do away with Jesus and thus to bring an end to the Jesus movement. In a sense the death on the cross is the price Jesus paid for his meal-fellowship with publicans and sinners. "Truly, it was under the shadow of the cross that Jesus ate and drank with the outcasts of his day."[13]

In Remembrance of Me

But Jesus wanted that the meal-fellowship with the poor and the marginalised should continue even after his going away. Jesus

---

[13] Kappen, *op.cit.,* 87.

wanted to assure the disciples that after his bodily departure from their midst he would continue to be present to them spiritually at the meal-fellowship; even more: he would be present at their meals in a uniquely *bodily* way. So at the last meal-fellowship with his close friends and disciples he broke bread with them and said: "Take and eat: this is my body given for you; do this in remembrance of me." (Lk. 22:19) What does this mandate really mean? What was Jesus referring to when he asked them to break bread *in remembrance* of him? Definitely there is a reference to the passion and death on the Cross.(I Cor. 11:26) . But a reflection on the *Sitz im Leben* of the last meal would take us to the meal-fellowship of Jesus with the publicans and sinners. We cånnot really grasp the deeper meaning of the *last meal* without relating it to the hundreds of occasions of Jesus having meal with the poor and the marginalised. In fact it is the praxis of having meal-fellowship with the *impure* that provoked the angry reaction of the religious authorities who forced Jesus to end his meal-fellowship movement with the last meal at that early age of his life.[14] Hence the mandate to come together and break bread *in remembrance* of Jesus would mean to continue the praxis of Jesus, ie. to continue the meal-fellowship with the poor and the marginalized; to re-*member* would mean really to receive the outcasts as members of one's own family. In this sense the words of Jesus at the last meal may be paraphrased thus:

You know why I am forced to bid farewell to you. With publicans and sinners we were having regular meal-fellowship. We broke bread with them, we spent time with them, we shared our life with them. They could then realise their human dignity, their worth as children loved by the heavenly Father. They felt that they were really the spiritual inheritors of the new order of the Kingdom of God. This was disturbing for those who built up their securities in the old order of religiosity. So they want to get rid of me. But I desire that our liberative praxis of the meal-fellowship continues. You should therefore come together and share meal with the poor

---

[14] Perrin,. Norman, Rediscovering the Teaching of Jesus, SCM, London, 1967, 102-105.

and the marginalised: share your life compassionately with them. Then be sure, I am in your midst in a *bodily* way; I am really present at your meal-fellowship. The bread that you break is truly *my body*. The cup that you share is filled with *my blood*. Like bread I am broken for you, so that broken like bread for one another you too may become my disciples. I have become bread for you, so that you too may become bread for others......

In order to make the disciples aware of this dimension of the breaking of the bread Jesus washed their feet like a slave (Jn.13:5). And the message is unambiguously given: "If I, your Lord and Master, have washed your feet, you must wash each other's feet. Do what I have done" (Jn. 13:14). It was definitely an emotionally dense moment in the life of the disciples. The message that was thereby communicated to them must have truly gripped them. Breaking of the bread in remembrance of the Master became a central event in the original praxis of the first Christian communities (Acts 2:46; 20:7,11; 27:35). Out of this intense experience evolved the praxis of the eucharistic sharing of the bread of the Lord. It was not a ritual practice, but the continuation of the meal-fellowship of Jesus. "The Eucharist has always carried the memory of Jesus' meals with tax collectors and sinners. Perhaps even more than the last supper of Jesus, what inspired the early Christian fellowship meals, which developed into the Eucharistic celebrations that we observe today, was the memory of the meals that Jesus ate with his outcast disciples."[15] Paul strongly admonishes the community in Corinth on this. The eucharistic assembly sharing the bread of the Lord should manifest the equality of all, the concern for the poor and the hungry (I Cor. 11:17-22). "A person who eats and drinks without recognising the Body of the Lord is eating and drinking to his own condemnation" (I Cor.11:29). To take part in the Eucharist is a grace and a responsibility: grace of feeling the *bodily* presence of the Lord in our midst, and the responsibility of breaking our life with others, especially with the poor and the marginalised. Only then can the Eucharist become a genuine continuation of the meal-fellowship of Jesus.

---

[15] Soares, *op.cit.,* 235.

The Church that Jesus envisaged may also be understood as the continuation of the meal-fellowship of Jesus with the poor and the marginalised. "The Church can become relevant and meaningful only if it becomes once again the table-fellowship of Jesus."[16] The sharing of meal with the outcasts has been a concrete expression of the way Jesus proclaimed the values of the Kingdom of God. In the meal-fellowship Jesus presented the model of the new order of realities, the new community he dreamt about. It is not the community in which one sits above the head of the other lording authority on others (Mk. 10:42), but one in which all sit on the same plane shoulder to shoulder and break the one bread with one another. It is the community in which one shares one's life with others in genuine love thus experiencing and communicating God's love that binds their hearts and transforms their lives. It is the community in which one realises that the Spirit of Christ breaks down the barriers which we humans put up on the basis of caste and race, religion and confession, cultural superiority and national pride (Gal. 3:28). It is the community in which the poor and the marginalised will be the first to be served for they are the *blessed* heirs of the new order.

Church is the continuation of the meal-fellowship of Jesus. Such a realisation would make us understand that the Church is primarily a spiritual movement and not an established religion: a movement *of* the Spirit, *in* the Spirit, *unto* the Spirit. Church is the community that is constantly alert to *what the Spirit of God is telling* here and now in the concrete situations of life. Church cannot just get settled as a religion called Christianity. Church and Christianity are not the same. The Kingdom of God and the Church are not the same. Church could be understood as the sacrament of the Kingdom of God, and Christianity is a socially and historically evolved format of the presence of the Church in the world. To be a disciple of Jesus is not identical with being a member of the religion of Christianity. Just being a Christian does not necessarily mean that one is a *disciple* of Jesus. Church is a spiritual communion;

---

[16] Kappen, *op.cit.,* 88

Christianity is an organised religion. Church as a movement of the divine Spirit permeates all religions and cultures. Christianity may establish itself as a religion parallel to the others. Church is the sacrament of the saving presence of God. Christianity is the culturally conditioned religious phenomenon. The spiritual dynamics of the Church may need the format of Christianity. But one can never forget that the Spirit constantly transcends the structures of every concrete religion, including Christianity. Church is a reality that is attentive to this power and presence of the Spirit in religions and cultures. In this sense the Church is a *mystical* reality with a self-transcending dynamic: alerting people to the mystery of the divine Spirit in their lives and cultures. And as a mystical reality and Spirit-generated movement the Church penetrates all religions and cultures and carves deeper into the divine depth of reality . "The Spirit explores the depth of everything, even the depths of God" (I Cor. 2:10). Church is a communitarian dimension of this transforming presence of the Spirit of God in the historical process and cultural creativity of humanity. In his meal-fellowship with the poor Jesus gave concrete expression to the presence of this Spirit; the Christian communities are called to continue this process so that the Church of Jesus' dream evolves within and beyond all religions.

Much has been said here on the negative attitude of the pharisees towards the meal-fellowship of Jesus. The pharisees are not just a group of religious conservatives of the time of Jesus. *Pharisee* is rather a religious archetype that can be found in any believer, at any time, in any religion whatsoever. It represents the tendency towards closing oneself within the traditional forms of religiosity without alertness to the new demands of the times and openness to the fresh ways of the working of the divine Spirit in the world. Pharisaism is a mind-set that refuses to allow transformation in one's life under the impact of the divine Spirit that constantly breaks down the fences which we humans put up in the name of religious heritage. Jesus' basic concern was to make people alert to the movements of the divine Spirit. Alertness to the Spirit makes one question the structures of social discrimination. The Spirit binds the hearts of people beyond all patterns of caste bias. Before God all humans are endowed with dignity and self-esteem. The meal-fellowship of Jesus was a place where people of all social strata and religions could experience the liberating presence of the Spirit. With this Jesus proclaimed a new ethos of human solidarity in contrast to the mind-set of pharisaism.

Christian Presence in India

What are the practical consequences of this perspective in the Indian context?

1. Society in India is characterised by a vibrant plurality of religions. Every religion has a spiritual dimension and a complex format of religious expression. The dialogue of religions should be sensitive to this depth dimension of spirituality. Those who believe in Christ the Saviour should then meet believers of other *paths* from within their Christ-experience. What is shared at this level is actually what the poor and the outcasts experienced with Jesus as he broke bread with them: the compassionate face of God. In fact all religions communicate God's mercy (*daya, karuna, rahamim, rahim)* in one way or other. When the disciples of Jesus meet the others in the spirit of the meal-fellowship of Jesus the Spirit of compassion binds the hearts of all on a common spiritual pilgrimage. Those who sat to dine with him came from diverse social strata, cultural backgrounds and religious affiliations. The meal-fellowship of Jesus is a Christian prototype of inter-religious fellowship. We can find similar motives of human solidarity in Hindu ashrams and Buddhist *sanghas.*

2. One of the forces at work in the Indian social fabric is the caste mentality. Individuals and groups are *graded* on the basis of birth (*janma*) and profession (*karma*), purity laws (*suddhi*) and inborn qualities (*guna*). That there are differences among individuals is a fact of life. But when these differences are attributed to insurmountable birth-bound factors and consequently individuals are discriminated, an oppressive social system evolves. Under different names discriminative factors are at work in all human societies all over the world. But in India a theological justification

is given to social stratification, as if the creator God wanted a caste-based society. As a result prejudices are injected into the religious psyche and caste-bias is built into the social fabric of India. This tragic situation needs a corrective: a spiritual vision based on the constitutive equality of individuals and dignity of persons. Jesus lived in a caste-ridden society and he opposed it through his meal-fellowship with the outcasts. The counter-cultural perspectives which evolve from this praxis of Jesus could be taken as an antidote to the exploitative caste mentality that disrupts social life in India. Christian communities have a significant role to play in overcoming the caste-based social structures. For this the Christian community itself has to be free of caste-bias. Church understood as the continuation of the meal-fellowship of Jesus offers a vibrant sign of the new culture of equality and human dignity. The *dalits* and the *harijans*, the outcasts and the marginalised sections should be able to find in the *spiritual* fellowship of the disciples of Jesus a home where they can experience integral liberation and social acceptance based on equality before the compassionate God.

3. The liberative praxis of Jesus has been a source of inspiration for many Christians in India in the last three decades to take creative steps of insertion into the milieu of the poor. Several lay organisations, especially those of the youth, insert themselves to the milieu of the downtrodden and work in solidarity with the *dalits* of the country. Quite a few religious Congregations have taken bold steps of living in the midst of the rural and urban poor sharing their lot and struggling with them for their rights. A lived experience of the exploited sections of the people has become an integral element of the formation of priests and religious in the Church in India. The ashrams of Christian initiative offer an atmosphere of genuine hospitality where people irrespective of caste and religion are welcome for spiritual pursuits and meal-fellowship. In the many projects and ministries of the Church *option for the poor* has become a normative factor. New initiatives like prison ministry, 'Birds of the Air', shelter homes, community with the handicapped, homes for the AIDS patients, palliative care for the terminally sick etc. show the face of a Christian community that gives witness to the

compassion of Christ. They all point to the new direction that the Church in India is taking under the inspiration of the meal-fellowship of Jesus and in response to the problems emerging from the struggles of the people. The great reform movements of India like the Sarvodaya movement of Mahatma Gandhi, anti-caste movements of Periyar, Ambedkar and Sahodaran Ayyappan, the Ezhava movement of Sree Narayana Guru and the Harmony movement of Basavanna have articulated their ideal of the egalitarian society in organising meal-fellowship with people of the diverse strata of society. In ashrams and Gurudwaras it is a normal practice to have shared meals with people of every caste and creed. In India to share meal with someone is a sign of accepting the other with respect and equality. The spirit of the meal-fellowship of Jesus resonates well with the counter-cultural ethos of some of the social liberative movements of the country.

4. If the origin of the Eucharist is to be found in the meal-fellowship of Jesus with publicans and sinners, a lot of radical questions come up on the theology and praxis of the Eucharist in the Christian communities. Over the centuries the breaking of the eucharistic bread has become a sacred ritual presided over by the priest. A believing community needs rituals for its coherence as well as symbols for its self-understanding. However the pristine inspiration of the Eucharist has to be explored beyond the realm of a ritual. Did Jesus want to institute a ritual? The concern of Jesus was to make his *bodily* presence felt in the community when they break bread with one another and share life with one another. And he gave a concrete example for this sharing of life in his meal-fellowship with the outcasts. A regular practice of sharing meal with the poor and insertion to the life of the marginalised would deepen the understanding of the mystery of the Eucharist in the Church. It will make us aware of the consequences which the Eucharist has in the life of individuals and communities. In fact the *real presence* of the suffering God is to be experienced on the face of the hungry and the thirsty, in the life of the poor and the outcasts, in the wounds of the humans and in the woundedness of the earth. "I was hungry, and you gave me food; I was thirsty, and

you gave me drink; I was a stranger and you gave me a welcome; I was lacking clothes and you clothed me; I was sick and you visited me; I was in prison and you came to see me. Whatever you did to one of the least of my brothers, you did to me." (Mt. 25:35-40). Eucharist is not just a ritual to be celebrated daily according to a pre-determined rubric, but primarily an invitation to break the body of Christ with the poor, to share life with the marginalized, to perceive the face of the suffering God on the faces of the suffering people. (Lk.10:37; Mt.5:23; 25:35). The *real presence* of Christ is to be experienced in the life and struggles of people; what we experience on the altar is the sacramental presence, that communicates the Christic dimension of life. Eucharist as the memorial of the passion, death and resurrection of Jesus is the sacrament of life in as much as it is intimately related to the divine dimension of the suffering and creativity of human persons.

5. There is a large section of Dalits in Indian society. (*Dalit* means the broken one). For generations this sector has been experiencing all sorts of oppression and discrimination based on birth-bound factors. Often the menial and dirty jobs are allocated to them, but they were not respected nor were they paid well for their service. They have been often denied admission to common places of worship, access to village wells and respectful treatment in public schools. In spite of the State regulations regarding reservations for Dalits in higher education and government offices, their plight continues to be sad. Though Christian community is based on egalitarian values, discrimination of dalits continues in several Christian communities. The meal-fellowship of Jesus may be taken as breaking bread with the dalits of his times. The publicans, the prostitutes, the lepers and the handicapped persons were the dalits of his country. These were really the *broken* sections of human life. The meal-fellowship was for them an experience of the healing presence of the Divine in their lives. If the Church is taken as the continuation of the meal-fellowship of Jesus, genuine concern for the dalits would become a hallmark of the Church in India. The presence of a Christian community would then mean a prophetic critique on the discriminative stance of society and a

powerful witness to the egalitarian values of Jesus. In the community of the Kingdom of God there can be no discrimination based on birth-bound factors or cultural bias.

Church as the continuation of the meal-fellowship of Jesus will evolve on the route of the struggles for equality and justice; Eucharist as the continuation of the meal-fellowship of Jesus would take place wherever life experiences brokenness and reconstruction.

7

THE VULNERABLE GOD

We all have an inborn idea of God, a sort of dictionary-definition of God: God is almighty, all-knowing and all-pervading; Creator of everything and Lord of all, ultimate source and final goal of our life. God is immanent and transcendent. In him we live and move and have our being. World religions communicate through a rich variety of symbols the experience of this God. Philosophy describes the reality of the Divine as Being-itself, as *motor immobilis*, mysterium *tremendum et fascinosum*. With all that we have a well-rounded image of God, a beautiful picture of God: God is the fullness of being and truth, goodness and love, beauty and power, *sat-chit-ananda*.

The Suffering God

With this beautiful image of God let us go up the hill of Calvary. There we stand before a man who hangs between heaven and earth. The *heaven* has apparently forsaken him, for he cries out: My God, my God, why have you forsaken me! (Mt. 27:46). The *earth* has abandoned him, for almost all his close friends have left him alone at this moment of agony. He could not come down from the cross; he was unable to *save himself*. (Mt. 27:42). The transcendent God above the heavens does not seem to respond to his cries, and the God within the cave of the heart does not seem to wake up. Here is a man who undergoes the deepest suffering of human beings: utter loneliness. With the eyes of faith we look deep into his tearful eyes, his bloodstained face, and confess: this is God's face turned towards the world. When we do that all our powerful images of God crumble and all the beautiful pictures of God turn into dust. Here we are confronted with the paradox of faith in the crucified God.

- We conceive an almighty God, but the cross reveals to us a God who is weak and feeble (I Cor. 1:25).

- We imagine an all-knowing God, but the cross unfolds the foolishness of God (I Cor. 1:25).

- We look up to heaven in search of the transcendent God, but here God meets us on the blood-stained paths of this earth.

- We meditate on a God resting within our heart, but God encounters us in the struggles of human life.

- We conceive a God who is enthroned above our heads as the Lord of all, but in Jesus God meets us as a slave waiting to wash our feet (Jn. 13:5).

- We imagine a God seated on the peak of this universe, but in Jesus God walks with us in this valley of tears.

- We contemplate God as the absolute beauty permeating the entire creation: but in Jesus God encounters us in the wounds of the humans and in the woundedness of the mother earth.

- We cry to the almighty God who has the power to remove all sufferings from this world within a moment, but on the cross we meet a God who himself becomes victim of the deepest suffering of human beings.

- We often ask, why God does not intervene at the atrocities committed by human beings, but the cross shows how God himself has become a prey to human cruelty.

In our frame of mind God the Lord of history is above history for he is beyond change and suffering; but the crucified God is God *within* history: God suffering with us. Here we meet God on the evolutionary paths of our life, stained with blood and tears, shaped by sweat and toil. The God revealed in the crucified Jesus is not the *motor immobilis* of philosophers, but the *emmanuel*, God with us in the shadows of suffering and death.

God's being is *becoming*; God's action is *passion*. God is a suffering God. This is the mystery and message of the cross of Jesus. God suffering ? How to reconcile these two terms? Human mind cannot in any way predicate suffering to God. This is something like trying to draw a circular triangle. Either circle or triangle; either God or suffering - both cannot go together! Here the logical pursuit of human reason reaches its boundary. It is a paradox to look at the crucified face of Jesus and discover there the face of God. Paul perceived this when he said: "The crucifixion of Christ cannot be expressed in the language of philosophy. The language of the cross is illogical..." (I Cor. 1:17). Yet this is the valid way of probing into the depth of the divine mystery. It is the way of the paradox, the way of *coincidentia oppositorum*.

The Two Basic Notions of God

Paul speaks of two basic types of God-seekers: the wise persons and the pious people:

Those who claim to be wise contemplate a God who is the fullness of being, the source and object of wisdom. The way to know this God is the philosophical pursuit of reason. But in reality God is beyond reason's comprehension: "I shall destroy the wisdom of the wise and bring to nothing the learning of the learned. Where are the philosophers now? Where are the teachers of the Law? Where are any of our thinkers today? Do you see how God has shown up the foolishness of human wisdom? It was God's wisdom that human wisdom should not know God" (I Cor. 1:19-21). In pursuit of human wisdom one tends to conceive God as the omniscient Absolute; but the cross reveals the apparent foolishness of God! This is unacceptable to philosophers; they would call it utter nonsense, folly and madness. Yet waking up in faith to the foolishness of God revealed in the crucified Jesus is a specificity of Christian faith.

The second type of God-seekers is the pious people, who in their popular forms of piety worship a God who is almighty: God has the power to intervene in the lives of people and events of history in a miraculous way in order to alleviate suffering and recreate life. Hence through devotional practices people pray ardently to this God, who works miracles and brings about healing. They will not believe 'unless they see signs and portents' given by an almighty God (Jn. 4:48). Their religious quest cannot be satisfied by a God who revealed his weakness on the Cross. For them therefore the message of the Cross is disappointing: absolute scandal, 'an obstacle that they cannot overcome' (I Cor. 1:23). Yet waking up in faith to the weakness of God revealed in the crucified Jesus is a specificity of Christian faith.

Paul invites us constantly to look at the face of the crucified Christ, in whom God's face was unveiled unto humanity. 'The only knowledge I claim to have is about Jesus, and about him as the crucified Christ" (I Cor. 2:2). "The only thing I can boast about is the cross of our Lord Jesus Christ" (Gal. 6:14). The cross of Jesus is the language of God's self-giving. It is not merely a past event of God's revelation, but an abiding language of God's self-manifestation. It is not merely a historical event of God's time-bound participation in human suffering, but the unfolding of a deep mystery of the divine reality here and now: the wound of the crucified Jesus is the revelation of the woundedness in God; the suffering of Jesus on the cross is the expression of the suffering in the inner-trinitarian life of the Divine. Crucified Christ is the embodied manifestation of *theopathy*. The death of Jesus is a statement of God about himself.[1]

Love Makes God Vulnerable

It has often been said: reason waits outside the gate, when love enters! Love is perhaps the only valid key for a deeper grasp of the mystery of God's suffering. Genuine love makes the lover vulnerable in relation to the beloved. An invulnerable person cannot love at all. Love is sustained by affectivity, i.e., one is deeply affected in encountering the beloved. Love therefore involves change, evolution, becoming, history. The unmovable mover cannot really love us, because love does not move him at all. An *almighty* God cannot really love us, because he does not need us, nor is he affected by our brokenness. Only of a God who is vulnerable, and who really suffers, can it be said: God is Love. "God suffers with

---

[1] Rahner, Karl SJ, *Sacramentum Mundi*, III-IV,1959, p. 208.

us far more than we suffer: we suffer for ourselves, God suffers for us."[2]

A scene from daily life may illustrate this mystery of love. The parents at home suddenly get the news that their little daughter on her way to school met with a traffic accident. How would the parents react to this? If they remain unaffected by the news it is evident that they do not really love their child. Parental love would impel them to put aside all other concerns and rush to the place to attend to the wounded child. The parents share the pain of the child. The entire family suffers with the suffering child. It is in this co-suffering that love enfleshes itself.

If God is love, God suffers with us. When there is such an amount of poverty and sickness, oppression and exploitation, violence and criminality of which millions are victims, can we think of God unaffected by all this suffering? Image of an invulnerable almighty God up in the heaven is a gruesome image of God. A God who has the omnipotence to intervene, and yet refuses to get involved in the tragic predicament of humanity, is a cruel God. Is it not this God of whom many God-seekers say, God does not exist? Atheism contains a valid critique on the ungodly images of God. When Jesus cried on the Cross in deepest agony, 'My God, my God, why have you forsaken me', did he not really experience himself being forsaken by the almighty God, whose omnipotence should have helped him 'come down from the cross'? At the same time Jesus experienced himself being loved and accepted by the Father God: 'Father, into your hands I commit my spirit' (Lk. 23:46). The God whom Jesus revealed is not the God of might but the God of love, not the God of omnipotence but the God of compassion: "the gentle Father and the God of all consolation, who comforts us in all our suffering, so that we can offer others, in their sufferings, the consolation that we have received from God ourselves" (II Cor.1:3-4). "When the crucified Jesus is called the 'image of the invisible God', the meaning is that this is God, and God is like this. God is

---

[2] Meister Eckhart, *Deutche Predigten und Traktate*, Josef Quint (ed), Diogenes, Munich, 1979, 131.

not greater than he is in this humiliation. God is not more glorious than he is in this self-surrender. God is not more powerful than he is in this helplessness. God is not more divine than he is in this humanity."[3]

What we experience in the crucified Christ is the truth that God suffers with us when we suffer, because God loves us. God has made our history of suffering into *his story* of passion; human history has become God's history with us. Jesus Christ is the enfleshing of the wounded love of God, the embodiment of the compassion of God, the manifestation of the motherliness of the Divine: the revelation of the suffering God. Only an affectionate mother can tell the child: 'come and drink from me' (Jn. 7:38). The divine fountain of life and love unfolded itself in Jesus Christ and hence he has become for us the well from which we can drink the water of divine Spirit" (Jn. 4:14; 7:39). "Jesus symbolised the heavenly mercy which makes all human suffering its own."[4]

The Compassion of Jesus

The life of Jesus has been a living testimony of God's compassion for the suffering people. He understood his call in terms of 'bringing Good News to the poor, proclaiming liberty to the captives, giving new sight to the blind, setting the downtrodden free and proclaiming the Lord's year of grace' (Lk. 4:18-19). He came as the Good Shepherd that is deeply affected when a single sheep is found lost (Lk.15:4). Jesus is the shepherd that undergoes the suffering of the lost sheep and surrenders his life for the sake of the sheep (Jn.10:11). As a hen gathers her brood under her wings he would protect the children of Israel (Lk. 13:34).

He lived with the poor and for the poor; he experienced intensely the struggles of the poor. He invited them to his meal-fellowship and broke bread - his life - with them. The sick, the brokenhearted, the blind, the cripple, the marginalised, the lepers, the exploited women, the forsaken children - these were close to

---

[3] Moltmann, Juergen, The Crucified God, SCM, London. 1979. 205.
[4] Tagore, Rabindranath, Towards Universal Man, New York, 1961, 172.

his heart. He called them 'blessed', for they were to experience God's compassion and inherit the new Kingdom. Suffering of people is the divine milieu in which Jesus communicated the experience of God's love. The healing experience of the poor and the sick is hailed as the primal sign of the Kingdom of God (Lk. 7:21). Jesus relativised creed, cult, code, community and all external forms of religiosity in favour of concern for the suffering human beings (Lk. 10:29-37, Mk. 3:1-6, Jn. 5:1-19, 8:1-11). This is powerfully brought out in the parable of the Good Samaritan (Lk.10:29-37)

In the world the suffering God continues to reveal his face on the wounded faces of the suffering people. God identifies himself with the suffering humanity: "I was hungry, I was thirsty, I was a stranger, I was naked, I was sick, I was in prison..." (Mt. 25:35-36). Only from the mouth of a vulnerable God can these words be heard. The decisive question on which our salvation is determined is this: are we able to see the face of God on the face of the suffering humans? Faith in the crucified Christ is a call to perceive God's presence in the wounds of human persons. In this sense the crucifixion of Christ is not just an event of the past, but a reality of the present: God-in-Christ still hangs on the cross. How can he come down from the cross when millions of human beings are still hanging on the cross!

Through the parable of the wounded father (Lk. 15:11-32) Jesus described the vulnerability of God the Father. When the younger son left the father's home he left a wound in the heart of the father. The father felt the pain of the son's departure because he loved the son. To love someone means to respect the freedom of the other and be prepared to be wounded by the other. Ever since the son left home the father was a wounded person. With a wounded heart he waited for the son's return. The father's unfailing love kindled fire in the heart of the son and he returned. Jesus described dramatically how unconditionally the father welcomed the son back home. As he saw the son coming from far he ran to him, clasped his hands, embraced him and took him back home with a joyful meal. The deeper message of the story is that God like a wounded father waits for the homecoming of all to the divine fatherly home. As long as there are sin and suffering in this world, we can only speak of a God who waits in agony. Until 'God will be all in all' we can only think of a suffering God, not of a God in glory. The glory of God is an eschatological reality in which the entire creation will participate (Rom. 8:21-25). Until this is realised Gods' being is *becoming*. Our life and struggle get meaning in working 'for the greater glory of God'.

Sin and Suffering

What is the cause of suffering in God? This is the unfathomable mystery of the 'depths of the Divine'. Biblical revelation tries to understand this mystery in terms of human freedom.

When God created the universe he found everything good, and the creator rejoiced in his creation. With the creation of the human pair God's ecstatic joy reached a climax, because 'God created male and female in the image of himself' (Gen. 1:27). God endowed the human persons with freedom to respond to his admonition on the 'tree of knowledge'. In realising this freedom the human pair responded in disobedience to the Creator, and sin entered creation causing alienation in humanity (original sin) and suffering in the entire creation. Did God the Creator remain unaffected by the sinful disobedience of the human persons? If God's creation is the outflow of his love, he cannot but be affected by the reality of alienation and suffering in creation. "In his mercy God suffers with us, for he is not heartless."[5] True love suffers the suffering of the beloved. The image of God that emerges in the subsequent books of the Bible is that of a vulnerable God: a God who 'walks with his people' as a good shepherd, 'takes them in his arms' as a father carries his child, 'writhes in pain' like a mother giving birth to her baby, suffers like a husband whose wife left him, gets angry and yet relents, feels remorse over punishing his people...(Is. 1:2-4; Jer. 4:19-22, 31:20, 42:10-11; Hos.2:1-3; 11:1-8). In fact the parable of the wounded father (Lk. 15:11ff) offers us a key to understand the

---

[5] Origen, Commentary on the Romans, 8.32.

mystery of God's suffering, which is the consequence of God's unconditional love in creating human beings in freedom. And God's suffering continues as long as human freedom disowns God.

Meaning of Resurrection

Does this mean that the entire purpose of God's creation is thwarted by the misuse of human freedom? Is human history tending towards a total tragedy? The answer to this existential theological question is given in the Resurrection of Christ. Cross reveals the vulnerability of God. What does Resurrection reveal?

The scene from our daily life depicted above may be helpful here. If the parents rushing to the child who met with an accident are so shocked by the event that they spend the whole time sitting near the child and grieving over it, the child is not helped. The parents would rather take the wounded child to the hospital and get proper medical attention in order to help the child get back to normal health. Love participates in the suffering of the other, and takes the initiative to remove suffering as well.

Love recreates what is destroyed and reassembles what is broken asunder. Love brings peace and instills hope. Love heals wounds and binds hearts together. Love enables one to forget the offence and forgive the other. Love opens the eyes to see the future always brighter than the past. Love reaches out to infinite horizons. Love is creative: it recreates everything anew, ever new.

This creative dynamics of God's Love has been made visible in the Resurrection of Christ. "The old is gone; everything is made new!" (II Cor. 5:17). God's Spirit is at work in our midst not only participating in our suffering, but also bringing about a new creation in all realms of our life. God's Spirit 'reconciles everything in and through Christ' towards the state when 'God will be all in all' (Col. 1:20; I Cor.15:28). At the end of times everything will be transformed into the *body* of Christ; we will be filled with the utter *fullness of God* (Eph.3:19). The entire creation is being progressively made transparent to the transforming presence of the Divine (Rom. 8:18-25).

Within and all around us there is a universal process of theophany: divine Light shines through everything. On the risen body of Christ we are graced to perceive this theophany, this total transparency of creation to the Creator. In this sense creation is moving towards a Christophany. Resurrection gives us an assurance that the world is moving towards final fulfilment in the Divine. Resurrection engenders in us the hope to await 'the new heaven and new earth, the place where righteousness will be established'(II Pet.3:13). Hope gives rise to courage and vision. Hence the farewell words of Jesus: "Fear not, I am with you always until the end of time!"(Jn.14:1; Mt.28:20). Resurrection is not just a fact of the past, but the reality of today: the luminous unfolding of the divine depth of reality. Christ is God-with-us here and now, shining upon us from the heart of the universe.

In the risen Christ God revealed his healing presence in the world, the recreating dynamism in the universe. Resurrection of Christ is the foretaste and assurance of the fulfilment of the world in the Kingdom of God. Resurrection gives us new eyes to see the world as the milieu in which the Kingdom of God takes shape in all realms of life. All our creative initiatives in life get thereby a divine horizon of meaning. Teachers enkindling light in the minds of students, nurses affectionately caring for the sick, social activists courageously promoting justice and harmony, farmers toiling hard to produce food for the hungry, factory workers giving shape to things needed for a better living, artists unfolding the beauty of creation, scientists exploring the mysteries of reality... all these who are committed to shaping a more humane and just society take part in the divine work of reconciling this world to God. Their spirituality consists in unfolding the sacred dimension of the secular. Resurrection has broken down the wall between the sacred and the secular.

Resurrection is the manifestation of the power of God: not the omnipotence, but the transforming love. God saves humanity not as an almighty God from above, but as the Saviour who takes part in our struggles and in our creative endeavours. Emmanuel - God is radically with us in our sufferings, and in our creative pursuits as well; God is with us as the crucified and risen Lord. A God who cannot suffer with us cannot really love us; a God who does not overcome the powers of suffering cannot save us. How can we call an invulnerable God our dear *Father*? How can a non-transforming God be our *Saviour*? Crucifixion and Resurrection are not just historical events of the past, but salvific realities of the present. They reveal the way God is with us in our midst here and now. They are the ongoing revelation of the vulnerability and creativity of God's love, expression of theo*pathy* and theo*phany*. In this sense the crucifixion of Christ continues in the sufferings of people, and the Resurrection of Christ still takes place wherever the world is created anew in the Spirit of the Kingdom of God.

Look deep into the wound of a wounded person and confess, *my Lord and my God!* - this is Christian contemplation. Get involved in the initiatives of integral liberation and feel, *God is with us* - this is Christian commitment.

8

EUCHARIST AS THE SACRAMENT OF THE EARTH

In the dominant world-views of today's science and technology, one tends to look at the earth merely as a *thing* to be used and even exploited. All that exists in and grows from the earth are considered to be objects of possession and consumption. The earth is objectified for scientific analysis and instrumentalised for technological development. Consequently we humans are getting increasingly uprooted from the earth and the earth itself is getting more and more sterile. In the spiritual perceptions of traditional Indian cultures, tribal and Vedic, there has been a world-view quite contrary to this. Earth is loved as the universal mother and the heavens looked upon as the cosmic father; rainfall was seen as heavens fertilizing the earth. The earth had been respected as the 'abode of the spirits', the 'bride of the heavens', the 'body of the Lord', the 'sheath of the Divine' and the 'form of the divine play' (*lila*). For centuries our people saw in the earth the fascinating and awe-inspiring manifestation of the divine power and presence. For them the earth was not so much an *object* to be used, as the life-giving *subject* of their existence: the earth is a sacred reality imputed with divine powers and healing energies. Through human labour the immanent potentialities of the earth are drawn out (*karshati*), and hence agriculture (*krishi*) was considered to be the unfolding of the earth through human creativity. Farming was conceived a sacred profession. Farmers venerated the earth as the all-embracing mother. Before laying hands on the plough the Vedic farmer would chant:

> Impart to us those vitalising forces,
> that come, O Earth, from deep within your body,
> your central point, your navel.

Purify us, O Mother, for we are your children.
Whatever I dig up of you,
may you of that have quick replenishment!
O Purifying one, may my thrust never
reach right unto your vital points, your heart.

(Atharva Veda, 12.1.12.35)

We are Earth

Earth is not just inert matter out there. It is rather the extended form of our body, and our body is transformed earth. The human body is earth waking to consciousness. When consciousness evolves through the earth, a human body takes shape. Humans are therefore offsprings of the mother earth. We are born of the earth, and we are constantly nourished by the earth. All the food that we eat - cereals and vegetables, fruits and pulses - are in fact products of the earth; these are just transformed earth! We *eat* the earth and share it with others. A loaf of bread is a lump of earth in an edible form. Food makes the nourishing energies of the earth - and of the universe - accessible to us.

Consumption of food means an intimate union with the earth, a deep communion with all things that grow out of the earth. Trees and plants are the feeding hands of the mother earth extended affectionately towards living beings. While eating we realize that we are like babies clinging on to the feeding breast of the one mother earth. In traditional cultures the time of eating and drinking has been considered a sacred moment. In most Indian families and communities we are used to eating in silence with certain rituals and prayers attached to dining. In the Bhagavad Gita (15:14), the consumption of food is understood as appeasing the divine fire (*vaisvanara*) in the body of living beings.

The food that we take, a self-gift of the earth, has a story to tell us. The bread that we eat has an autobiography to narrate. Jesus alludes to this with the metaphor of the grain of wheat (Jn. 12:24). The grain surrenders its provisional security and lets itself fall on the earth. It allows itself go through a painful process of brokenness and death. In this process it recapitulates within itself the destiny of everything that lives and dies and is reborn. As it dies, the life-giving energies of the earth penetrate through the little grain and stir up new life. Slowly the mother earth transforms herself into the plant and rises towards the heavens, the father of all. In a sense every plant is a resurrection of the earth unto new life. From far and near it absorbs the vitalising energies: from sun and moon, from rain and wind, from the hidden springs of the earth as well as from the vibrations of the ether-space. All these are transformed into the vital sap of the plant which thus grows as a fountain that lets the life-giving elixir of the earth stream forth. And in an auspicious season the plant gives birth to thousands of grains.

Each plant is a microcosm and each grain is an embodiment and receptacle of cosmic energies. Hence it contains a tremendous potential for nourishing life. Once the grains are ripe, they are harvested, dried, processed and made ready for becoming food for others. Here again the grains go through a painful process - the second moment of death - this time not in the generative warmth of the earth but in the transforming heat of the fire, another cosmic element. The cosmic fire that drew them out of the womb of the mother earth now transforms them to a new existence. The small grains become bread, source of life and nourishment for living beings. Bread is further broken, chewed and digested. Bread becomes our body. Earth transforms itself into our body.

Only with great devotion and genuine gratitude can we eat food. Besides the story of the earth described above, the bread also tells us the story of human labour. The sweat of farmers, the work of merchants and the labour of bakers have all gone into the formation of bread, into the transformation of the earth. Along this process women, men and even children have toiled hard to prepare the bread on the table. Bread embodies the collaboration between the earth and the humans, the communion between matter and spirit, the harmony between nature and culture. It is through human labour that the fertilizing energies of the earth evolve into food. Bread is at the same time 'fruit of the earth and work of human hands'. Through labour the human body nourishes the earth and brings it to full blossoming; and the earth in turn nourishes the human body by rendering food materials. There is a mutually nourishing relationship between the earth and the humans (Bhag.Gita, 3:11). Food is the crystallization point of the relatedness of the human body with the earth. In the sweat of human labour earth produces grains; grains become bread; bread is turned to our body, and our body in turn nourishes the earth - this is the cyclic process of life (*yajna*) which we experience daily. God enters into this process and meets us on this life-line - this is the Eucharist!

The Earth is Sacred

It is significant that Jesus chose bread and wine, fruit and juice of the earth, for mediating his abiding presence in a tangible way unto the end of times. With this Jesus brings us to the awareness of the mystery of the presence of the Divine in the womb of the earth, in human labour and in human solidarity that makes the earth generate food. The Eucharist reveals the presence of the Lord not only in the believing community but also in the cosmic realities of which the earth is the primal element. Hence the Eucharist evokes our responsibility not merely to one another, but to the earth as well.

To break the Eucharistic bread means to break our life with one another and for the mother earth too. The Eucharist reminds us that 'the earth belongs to the Lord' (Lev 25:23) and that he has entrusted it to us as a gift and as a responsibility, as *datum* and *debitum*, to be nourished by it and to nourish it as well. We are commissioned to 'cultivate the earth and to take care of it' (Gen. 2:15). The Eucharist makes us realise that our earth is the earth of the covenant, for God has covenanted the earth to himself. Sharing of the eucharistic bread with one another means also a call to share the earth with one another in justice and solidarity, and not to hold it greedily in possession. Eucharist is the sacrament of the earth.

The Eucharist is therefore the revelation of the universal theophany, which we Christians experience as Christophany. In the Eucharist we experience the unfolding of the presence of Christ hidden in the womb of the earth. The hymn at the beginning of the Gospel according to John gives us an insight into this experience.

The entire universe has been created in and through the divine Logos. "He is the Life of the world!" (Jn.1:4). The divine Logos is therefore the immanent life-giving principle of the universe. In every atom, there is the vibration of the Logos; in every living cell there is the throbbing of the Logos. "Nothing that exists can exist except in and through the Logos" (Jn. 1:3,10). The Logos is the divine wellspring within the womb of mother earth. Nature is the bearer of the Sacred. Earth is the body of God. We are standing perpetually on a holy ground. "The sacramental presence of the Spirit endows all of creation with a sacred value and dignity."[1]

Reality is vibration - this is the great insight of the modern age. What we sense as solid matter is not really solid, but a definite moment in the mutual compenetration of millions of subatomic vibrations. There is nothing really static in the universe; everything is in a constant flux, in a continuous process of evolution: *being is becoming*. In the throbs of energy which make up the universe the Greek sages perceived the power of the Logos. In the ethereal vibrations which energise the universe the vedic seers sensed the power of the divine sound OM. In the continuous flux that brings about cosmic harmony the Chinese masters experienced the interplay of yin-yang. If matter is energy, the vibrations evolve ultimately from a divine sphere. The ultimate immanent energy-source of this cosmic process is the divine Spirit. The heartbeat of matter is the divine Logos.

The discovery of modern physics is that the constitutive subatomic structure of our body - and of the entire cosmos - is 99.99% a vacuum field! There is actually only a minimal portion of matter in our body, and in the universe. For the most part we are of a spiritual energy. The knowledge communicated through our physical senses causes a sort of illusion (*maya*) about the reality. We are not what we think, we are. We are not our own property! Through the spiritual insights, like the Pauline one, we realize that our body is the *temple of the Spirit* (I Cor. 6:20), that this universe is the body of the Lord. Such a perception gives a divine dignity to the human body and a sacred meaning to the earth.

---

[1] Nash, James A, Living Nature, Abingdon, Nashville 1991, 115.

The Eucharist initiates us to the realization that our body - the earth and the entire universe - is the evolving body of the Lord, in which the divine Spirit (*ruach, pneuma, atman*= breath) breathes. The real change that takes place on the eucharistic table is the sacramental expression of the great change that is continuously taking place on the earth: all things are being made into the body of the Lord, i.e. all are made increasingly transparent to the glory of the Lord. "All things are being progressively reconciled to God through Christ, in the Spirit" (Col. 1:20; Rom. 8:23). At the end everything will be 'filled with the utter fullness of God" (Eph. 3:19). And finally 'God will be all in all.' (I Cor. 15:28)

The Indian psyche resonates well with this experience of the cosmic immanence of the Divine. The tribals have a keen sensitivity to perceive the Great Spirit in all realities of nature. The Vedic seers chanted the praises of the Divine in the fertilizing power of the earth (*prithivi*) , in the refreshing flow of the water (*apah*), in the purifying energy of the fire (*agni*), in the enlivening movements of the wind (*vayu*) and in the integrative vibrations of the cosmic space (*akasa*) . They lived in harmony (*rta*) with the universe. The Upanishadic sages perceived the divine Self (*Atman*) at the core of reality. The Atman the Ground of Being (Tait. Up. 3.1) is 'hidden in the heart as well as in the highest heaven' (Tait. Up. 2.1); hence the entire universe is the 'body of the Atman' (Mundaka Up. 2.1.4). The divine Self "pervades the entire realm of reality like butter in milk" (Svet. Up. 1.16). The Bhagavad Gita describes that the divine Lord is present at 'the heart of all things', as their 'source of life', as their 'inner light' and 'final goal' (15:15, 7:9, 13:18). In fact the entire universe is like a tree that constantly grows out of the 'undying divine seed' (7:10).

The immanence of the Divine is not a static presence. Its dynamism actualizes the universe and holds every atom, every living cell, in a constant movement. Its binding force keeps all cosmic realities in deep inter-connectedness. The divine Atman is the axis of the ever rotating cosmic wheel. The entire realm of reality is the dance of the divine Lord. The dancing Siva is a powerful icon of the cosmic dance of the Divine within the vibrant space of the atom as well as in the orbit of the galaxies. We humans participate in this dance consciously. Human labour gets its divine significance in the sense that it is an integral element of the rotation of the cosmic wheel (*yajnachakra*). Human creativity makes the cosmic wheel rotate. Vedic rituals are meant to be the celebration of human participation in this cosmic process of harmony (*dharmachakra*). Rituals promote cosmic well-being which in turn nourishes the humans for offering rituals. (Bh. Gita, 3:14). The real meaning of the rituals consists not in the cultic performance but in tuning our life to that of the Divine.(Bh. Gita, 9:26-27). A work that is done without clinging on to the ego (*nirahamkara*) is a work done as sacrifice (*yajna*). What one sacrifices is the greedy clinging on to one's ego. "The work that is done without attachment but in inner freedom, out of an integral experience of reality, can be called *yajna*; this alone leads to integration"(Bh. Gita, 4:23).

In the Samkhya philosophical system matter (*prakrti*) is considered as the feminine receptacle and body of the generative spiritual principle (*purusa*). In the later advaitic-jnana tradition Brahman is experienced as the all-embracing reality, and in the dvaitic-bhakti traditions the cosmos is conceived as the body of the personal Lord (*isvara*). The popular bhakti poets of India sang out of an ecstatic experience of 'seeing the Lord in all things'. The symbol-rich rituals of Indian religions and the colourful dances of Indian cultures celebrate the awareness of the cosmic presence of the Divine. In short the Indian mind is spontaneously attuned to the contemplation of the Divine in the manifold realities of the cosmos. Rabindranath Tagore spells out this spiritual attitude to nature very beautifully:

> Day after day, O Lord of my life, shall I stand before Thee face to face.
> With folded hands, O Lord of all worlds, shall I stand before Thee face to face.
> Under Thy great sky, in solitude and silence, with humble heart, shall I stand before Thee face to face
>
> (Geetanjali, no. 76).

The Paschal Mystery of the Earth

The Eucharist can be understood as a Christian celebration of the mystique of nature. At the core of the Christian faith lies the experience: the Logos became flesh. From within the womb of the earth the divine Logos unfolded itself in a concrete human body. A small portion of earth thus became the transparent medium of the self-unfolding of the divine Logos in the world: he dwelt in our midst (Jn. 1:14). In the Christian experience Jesus of Nazareth is the concrete embodiment of the Logos, the face of God turned towards humanity. In and through him we experience the *way* to the divine Ground of being, the *truth* of the divine mystery of reality and the *life* of the hidden divine springs. Faith in Jesus as the Christ would then mean an invitation to perceive the power and presence of the Logos in the earth, and in all things which embody themselves from within the earth.

In the light of the Christ experience we can look at the earth as the body of the Lord. Body is a powerful symbol that articulates not only the deep immanence of the Logos in the universe, but also the interconnectedness and mutual interdependence of all beings. Modern physics has scientifically proved that everything is connected to everything else in an incredibly complex network. "In fact, the atoms and molecules that constitute the bread and wine we use today are indistinguishable from those that made up that loaf and cup that Jesus blessed at the Last Supper."[2] In as much as Christ is the revelation of the Logos, theophany becomes Christophany. "All things in heaven and on earth have been created in and through him, and unto him" (Col. 1:15-7). "I have experienced the Diaphany of the Divine at the heart of a glowing universe through contact with the Earth: the Divine radiating from the depths of a blazing Matter."[3]

The death of Jesus is a radical entry of the Divine into the brokenness of the earth and the Resurrection of Christ is the total

---

[2] Cummings, Charles, Fruit of the Earth, Fruit of the Vine, in: Albert J. LaChance (ed), Embracing the Earth, Orbis, New York, 1994, 159.

[3] Teilhard de Chardin, Pierre, The Heart of Matter, Translated by Rene Hague. Collins, London, 1978, 16.

transformation of the earth into the *new* earth. Faith in the salvific events of Jesus' death and resurrection is a deeper entry into the paschal mystery of the earth. The presence of God in the world - in the earth and in humanity - is a suffering and transforming presence: God suffers with the mother earth and transforms her to the new creation. In the wounds of the crucified Jesus we see the wounds of the earth and in the light of the risen Christ we see the glory unto which the earth is waking (Rom. 8:22-25).

> "When the vessel of his body was shattered in death, Christ was poured out over the cosmos: he became actually, in his very humanity, what he had always been in his divinity: the very centre of creation."[4]

Hence in the brokenness of the earth we see the presence of God's brokenness for us, and in the re-creative dynamics of the earth we sense the presence of God renewing all things. The Eucharist as the memorial of the paschal mystery of the Lord is a celebration of the paschal mystery of the mother earth. In the broken bread we perceive the brokenness of the earth that God has entrusted to our care. And in this broken bread the Lord meets us from within the heart of the earth. The events of the incarnation, death and resurrection, as well as their sacramental celebration in the Eucharist, are to be understood as the salvific process which is truly a process in the earth. The earth is integrally related to the salvific event revealed in Jesus the Christ. This is implied in the belief in the resurrection of the body. At the end God will be all in all: the entire earth will be made transparent to the divine Spirit, will be converted to the glorified body of Christ. "In Jesus Christ the earth does indeed become the face of God and the place of saving encounter. In Jesus' resurrection the earth, which has seen and borne in its bosom so much death and decaying, finally transcends death and attains abounding and endless life. In Jesus the earth has become supremely honored, seated as it is at the right hand of God."[5]

---

[4] Rahner, Karl, On the Theology of Death, Herder, New York, 1962, 66.
[5] Rayan, Samuel, SJ, The Earth is the Lord's, in: David Hallman(ed), Ecotheology, Voices from South and North, Orbis, New York, 1994, 138.

The Spirit of the risen Christ is working in all realms of life to 'restore them in Christ', to bring them under the dominion of God. The entire earth is thus progressively brought to a theophany. Human labour is a participation in the re-integrative work of the divine Spirit. In all the labour done in solidarity with one another to evoke the fertilizing energies of the earth, in all the work performed to nourish and protect mother earth, in all the initiatives taken to preserve the beauty and well-being of the earth, we collaborate with and in the divine Spirit that brings about universal harmony. When the farmers' sweat falls on the earth and arouses the generative energies of the earth there is a moment of resurrection: the Spirit that raised Jesus into a new body raises the earth to the new earth.

When in the believing community the bread, fruit of human labour on the earth, is raised to be the body of Christ, there is a moment of resurrection too: the Spirit that is at work in the process of the earth changes the bread into the body of Christ thus revealing the emerging universal theophany. The Eucharist points to the truth that the earth and all that grows out of the earth are made increasingly transparent to the divine Spirit: they are transformed into the body and blood of Christ. They are being 'freed from the slavery to corruption and brought into the glorious freedom of the children of God'. (Rom. 8:21) "The Eucharist is that visible point in the cosmos towards which the crucified Christ - now that he is 'lifted up from the earth' in glory (Jn. 12:32) - is constantly drawing everything from every corner of the universe."[6] The Eucharist is that sacramental centre of the new creation. The Eucharist unfolds the truth that the entire world is a sacrament. "If I firmly believe that everything around me is the body and blood of the Word, then for me is brought about that marvelous 'diaphany' which causes the luminous warmth of the single life to be objectively discernible in and to shine forth from the depths of every event, every element."[7]

---

[6] Cummings, Charles, Fruit of the Earth, Fruit of the Vine, in: Albert J. LaChance (ed), Embracing the Earth, Orbis, New York, 1994, 157.

[7] Teilhard de Chardin, Pierre, op.cit. 127

After partaking in the body of Christ at the Eucharist one should be able to look at everything that sprouts forth from mother earth and say with Christ: *this is my body*. The seedling, plants, trees, flowers and fruits are in a sense the body of Christ. The hills, mountains, rivers, seas and the entire galaxy are somehow parts of the cosmic body of Christ. And after drinking from the cup of the blood of Christ at the Eucharist one should be able to see the sweat and tears which fall on the earth, the pouring of innocent blood on this earth, and say with Christ : *this is my blood*. In poverty and sickness, in injustice and exploitation, the blood of Christ is being continuously shed. In the silent groaning of the earth wounded by human greed and insensitivity the wounds of Christ are still bleeding. The Eucharist is the sacramental manifestation of the hidden presence of Christ in the cosmos, in the wounds of the earth as well as the human initiatives for the creation of a new earth. The eucharistic body and blood of Christ is the *ekstasis* of the Divine on the earth, the sacramental unfolding of the cosmic body of Christ. What happens on the eucharistic table is the sacramental expression of what has been happening in the earth. St. Ireneus states : "The Lord declares that the wine, which is part of creation, is his own blood and makes it the nourishment of our blood; he declares that the bread, which is also part of creation, is his own body and makes it the nourishment of our body." (Adv. Her., 5.2.2.)

The death and resurrection of the Lord continues in the evolution of the earth. *Emmanuel,* God is with us in the passion and resurrection of mother earth. "The body of Christ that the Christians eat and drink is in fact the real eating and drinking of the cosmic body and blood of the divine One present in every atom and every galaxy of our universe... And if Jesus Christ is Mother Earth crucified, then the eating and drinking at the Eucharist is the eating and drinking of the wounded earth."[8]

The understanding of the Eucharist as the sacrament of the earth has two significant consequences: one in the celebration of the Eucharist, and the other in our attitudes towards the earth.

---

[8] Fox, Matthew, The Coming of the Cosmic Christ. Harper, New York, 1988, 214.

Celebration of the Eucharist

As the sacrament of the earth the Eucharist reveals that the earth is the body of the Lord. If so, the celebration of the Eucharist should also be a celebration of the earth: thanksgiving for what the earth is for us and a reminder of what we should be for the earth. In the religious rituals of Indian heritage - both of the primal cultures and of Hinduism - the earth has an important place. The tribals have their rituals in sacred groves or on agricultural fields. These are often associated with the processes of the earth: fertility, germination, first-fruits and harvesting. In Hindu traditions the altar made of stone carved out of the earth is installed on the earth. The devotees pay homage to mother earth by prostration and receives her blessing by devoutly touching the earth with both hands and then placing the hands on the forehead. They bring fruits and flowers, cereals and grain; the priest places them on the altar as expressions of their self-gift to the Lord in deep gratitude for the life-giving energies of the mother earth (*prthivi*). Pure water (*apas*), the juice of the earth, is profusely used for purification and libation. Different forms of incense and fine-smelling pastes evoke the experience of the life-giving breath (*prana*) of the earth. The entire ritual revolves around the sacred fire (*agni*) that is kindled from within the heart of the earth, for it is sparked by the rubbing of two stones or wooden pieces (*arani*). The rhythmic chanting and the vibrations of the gong put the worshippers in harmony with the space within and above the earth (*akasa*). Thus the ritual awakens the devotees to a consciousness of the entire cosmos of which they are integral parts, and to which they have a sacred responsibility.[9] The ritual enables them to see 'that everything is permeated by the divine Self', and to perceive that the earth is the 'body of the Lord' (Bhag. Gita, 4:24, 6:30). *Padasparsam kshamasva me* - forgive me, mother earth, for keeping my feet on your breast - this is the morning prayer with which a devotee would begin the day. Much can be learned from this Indian heritage for celebrating the Eucharist as the sacrament of the earth in a more meaningful and attractive way.

---

[9] Painadath, Sebastian SJ, Hindu Rites of Passage and the Christian Sacraments, in: The Way Supplement 94 (1999): 131-40.

The cosmic symbols and earthbound postures would immensely help to evoke a sense of union with the Divine present in the earth. Rhythmic chanting and dance can be a means for the eucharistic community to experience resonance with the entire universe.[10]

Concern for the Earth

Such a cosmic celebration of the Eucharist leads to a change of our attitudes to nature. The earth and all that grows out of its womb cannot just be looked upon as objects of conquest and consumption: the earth is rather the subject of our existence, the source of all the vital energies as well as the extended form of our body. "The subject-object mode of thinking is not suitable for the question regarding our dealing with nature."[11] It is in the dominant culture of the *left* half of the brain that we are forced to objectify the earth and use it for scientific explorations. The Eucharist however opens our eyes to a contemplative perception of reality with the *right* half of the brain. Then the Eucharist unfolds the divine mystery of life and its celebration gets a mystical character. When one wakes to the eucharistic mystique of the earth, to the realization that the earth is actually the body of Christ, one develops an attitude of compassion and concern for the earth. This perception offers an ecosophy, 'wisdom of the earth'. It is the awareness of the constitutive interrelatedness between the earth and human beings in the divine Spirit. It is the mystical intuition of the universal theophany, that everything is ultimately the unfolding of the ONE. Ecosophy is the realization of the universal symbiosis: all beings are bound together in the one evolutionary process of life.[12]

The Eucharist makes one realize that human labour is not just a technological manipulation of the earth but a creative and

---

[10] Painadath, Sebastian, SJ, Verwandlung des Leibes, in: Der Geist reißt Mauern nieder, Kösel, Munich, 2002, 105-108.

[11] Panikkar, Raimundo. Oekosophie, der kosmotheandrische Umgang mit der Natur, in Hans Kessler (ed), Okologisches Weltethos im Dialog der Kulturen and Religionen, Darmstadt, 1966, 62.

[12] Painadath, Sebastian SJ, Ecosophy, Lessons from Indian's Spiritual Heritage, in: Joseph Mattam (ed), Ecological Concerns, An Indian Response, NBCLC, Bangalore, 1998, 102.

contemplative involvement with the earth in order to bring it to full blossoming. The eucharistic perspective on earth does not make us unproductive but evokes all the creative human energies in the process of the unfolding of the earth: the individual is thereby integrated to the totality of the earth's evolution, into the fullness of becoming *the body of Christ*. The Eucharist then becomes a divine critique of the patriarchal modes of *subduing* the earth (Gen. 1:28) and promotes a rather maternal approach of *caring* for the earth (Gen. 2:15). If the earth is our life-giving mother, we are also called to be the caring mothers of the earth. The Eucharist as the sacrament of the earth articulates also the anger of the mother earth - and the anger of God as well - on all that destroys the life-nourishing springs of the earth: devastation through radioactive and chemical wastes, poisonous effluents and emissions from factories as well as the destruction of forests and depletion of water resources. The Eucharist can thus be taken as a sacrament of protest in the context of today's technocratic civilization, capitalist economy and global consumerist culture. If the earth is the body of the Lord, the Lord does care for the earth; he does not want his body to be devastated and made sterile. Human labour that takes strength and motivation from the Eucharist would mean participation in the caring work of the motherly divine Spirit on the earth. To receive the body and blood of the Lord at the eucharistic table means to commit oneself to the transformation of the earth into the body of the Lord.

Teilhard de Chardin experienced this cosmic significance of the Eucharist powerfully and articulated it succinctly:

> Lord, since I have here neither bread, nor wine, nor altar, I will make the whole earth my altar and on it I will offer you all the labours and sufferings of the world.... I will place on my paten, O God, the harvest to be won by this renewal of labour. Into my chalice I will pour all the sap which is to be pressed out this day from the earth's fruits. My paten and my chalice are the depths of a soul laid widely open to all the forces which in a moment will rise up from every corner of the earth and converge upon the Spirit... Over every living thing, which is to spring up to grow, to flower, to ripen during this day I say again the words : This

is my Body. And over every death-force which waits in readiness to corrode, to wither, to cut down, I speak again your commanding words which express the supreme mystery of faith : This is my Blood.[13]

---

[13] Teilhard de Chardin, Pierre, op.cit. 119-123.

The Inward Journey

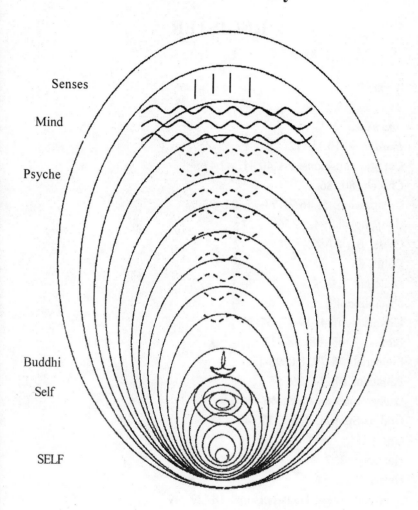

REGISTER